FAMILY
INTEGRATION
AND MENTAL
HEALTH
Au-Deane S. Cowley

San Francisco, California
1978

Published By

R & E RESEARCH ASSOCIATES, INC.
4843 Mission Street, San Francisco, California 94112

Publishers

Robert D. Reed and Adam S. Eterovich

Library of Congress Card Catalog Number

78-62234

I.S.B.N.

0-88247-539-8

ACKNOWLEDGMENTS

Sincere appreciation is extended to Dr. Robert M. Gray, Committee Chairman, for his encouragement, supervision and rigorous expectations that he maintained throughout the formulation and completion of this study. I also wish to acknowledge his sponsorship on my behalf for the NIMH Research Fellowship which I received for the academic year 1969-1970. To Supervisory Committee members Dr. Wen Kuo, Dr. Marlene Lehtinen, Dr. Rex A. Skidmore and Dr. Ted C. Smith go appreciation and thanks for their support, encouragement and sound criticisms. A special thank you is extended to Mike Lemming and Dr. Fred V. Janzen for consultation, and to Dr. Glenn M. Vernon and Dr. Ray R. Canning for serving on my initial graduate committee. I'd also like to acknowledge the expertise of my typist, Gay Burkholz.

In addition to these significant others whose visible input into this project has been acknowledged, it only seems appropriate that as a preface to this study on Family Integration and Mental Health, that I also acknowledge the impact on me of both my family of orientation and my family of procreation.

From my first family -- parents Earl Budge and Jhoun Chugg Shepherd -- and siblings -- Winona, Ramona, Phillip and Helen -- came a foundation that offered both stimulation and support. My spouse, Carter Wallace

Cowley, has encouraged me and made available the psychic space that is required if one is to continue to grow. Each of our children has introduced me to new dimensions of life and broadened my understanding of inter-personal relationships, communication, and the awesome responsibility of parenthood. To David, Cardeane, Michael and Phillip go my appreciation for their acceptance and support of a "mod mom". Without the good natured encouragement and willing help of my family members, this project and the preceding two degrees would have been much more difficult to accomplish.

TABLE OF CONTENTS

Page

LIST OF TABLES AND FIGURES

CHAPTER I

INTRODUCTION

Statement of the Problem

As the most pervasive and basic aspect of human environment, the family has long been regarded as a prime index of the mental health of individuals as well as of societies. More specifically, the impact that the quality of life within a specific family has upon the psychological development and well-being of its members has been the subject of much research interest. Since mental illness continues to be a major health problem, studies into the etiology of psychological impairment are certainly warranted. The purpose of this study was to explore the association between family integration and the prevalence of psychological stress that may lead to the development of psychiatric symptoms in heads of households.

Although many studies have attempted to assess the role of various internal processes in the psychological organization or disorganization of the family and the mental health of its members, many gaps remain. Not enough consensus has been obtained to allow family theorists to state with any certainty just what the role of the family is with regard to human adaptation and personality integration, or to predict what psychological effects differing kinds of interaction and stress levels within the family will have upon the mental health of the members therein. For example, does living in a poorly integrated family expose family members to more stressful interaction than living in a well integrated family? Does the quality of family life play a larger part in determining future psychological functioning than other social-demographical factors? Is it more detrimental to mental health to remain in a poorly integrated family, or to divorce? Does family failure not terminated by divorce, death, or separation have a differential impact on the two sexes? It is to these kinds of questions that this study has been directed.

Interactional Focus

Traditionally, psychiatrically based studies have viewed the mentally ill person as an organism and paid scant research attention to the total person as he develops within a specific social milieu. During the past decade, however, researchers from various disciplines within the field of mental health have given increased and systematic attention to the effects of broad socio-cultural factors on the prevalence of mental illness and more specifically to exploring the role that the total family system may have in fostering the development of psychiatric symptoms in its individual members. There has now been developed a considerable body of research in which the significance of the family's psychological environment is recognized in the prevention, cause and treatment of individual mental illness (Glasser and Glasser, 1970, p. 328).

2

Haley (1971) has written about the shift in focus from the individual (e.g., intrapsychic state) to the relationships (e.g., interpersonal systems) in which the person is embedded in making psychiatric diagnoses (Haley, 1971, p. 225). Meissner (1964) also has observed the trend toward viewing the individual family member who is mentally ill as being a manifestation of pathological familial interaction. He wrote:

> It is generally agreed that the family itself is the locus of resident pathology and that the patient is somehow externalizing and experiencing symptomatically the underlying disturbance within the family (p. 21).

These psycho-social approaches to understanding family factors which influence human behavior are based on the assumption that people do not have problems but are a part of a system that has problems. This view is corroborated by findings of Tharp and his co-workers (Crago and Tharp, 1968; Tharp and Otis, 1966) who found that one observes psychopathology only when the conflict is produced by the absence of satisfying role reciprocations (Lipetz, 1971, p. 342). In line with these kinds of observations, the main focus of this study is to test out whether the lack of healthy integration within a family could produce a psychological environment wherein basic human interactional needs are not adequately met and hence conditions created which could lead to the dysfunctional adjustment of family members in terms of mental well-being.

Certainly, there are other models for viewing human behavior within the family besides the interactional or interpersonal-systems approach.

Increasingly, however, the scientific thrust in studying families seems to be moving in the direction of trying to assess the quality of life within a particular family system, and then delineating the factors that seem to make that system functional or dysfunctional for the mental and emotional well being of one or more of its members (Hill, Moss and Wirth, 1953; Ackerman, 1961; Weinberg, 1967; Henry, 1971; Satir, 1972).

That quality of family life and the development of psychiatric symptoms in family members are inter-related seems clearly supported by the literature in the areas of mental health and family studies. The task remains, however, for the researcher to discover just how much of the variance in the dependent variable of psychiatric symptoms can be explained by family factors. Theories emphasizing constitutional endowments, social components, or physiological dysfunction are not to be denied, but in this study the research focus is on the interactional antecedents of psychological stress that precede mental illness. The unit of study is therefore the socialized person living within a family system.

Theoretical Foundation of the Study

In the interest of research into the realities of family life and of theory building, Hill and his collaborators have been most responsible for isolating, labeling, and describing the five major frameworks for family study which are: (1) the institutional approach, (2) the structural-functional approach, (3) the interactional approach, (4) the situational approach, and (5) the developmental approach (Hill and Hansen, 1960).

Among these five major frameworks, one area of focus within family studies, and a framework frequently used as a base for research by American sociologists is the area of internal relationships between family members, or the interactional approach. Early contributors to this theoretical framework are Cooley, Park, Mead, Thomas, and Burgess (Christensen, 1964, p. 9). Currently, the "psychosocial interior of the family" as an area of focus is quite prominent among students of the family:

> This means that attention is most fully given to what the family is to and for itself and its members rather than what it is to and for the larger society. The psychosocial interior is that region of the universe where the members of a family meet and make a life together. It is a region of the mind, that "place" where there is a meeting of minds primarily in the sense of individual selves confronting, engaging, and being struck off from one another, rather than in the usual sense of reaching agreement through rational discussion (Handel, 1967, pp. 1-2).

It is within the family interaction conceptual approach to the study of the family with its emphasis on the "internal workings" of the family and the "formative powers" of the family that this research found its rationale. This particular approach to family study received its first clear conceptualization in the mid 1920's when Burgess described the family as a "unity of interacting personalities":

> The interactional approach has developed from the fields of sociology and social psychology. It began about the middle of the 1920's when Ernest W. Burgess, a follower of George Herbert Mead and a symbolic interactionist, first described "the family as a unity of interacting personalities." It strives to interpret family phenomena in terms of internal processes, role playing, status relations, communication problems, decision making, stress reaction, and the like. Within this approach, little attempt

is made to view the over-all institutional or cross-cultural or transactional relationships of the family considered as a unit in society (Christensen, 1964, p. 22).

Those most instrumental in applying general assumptions of the interactional approach into more specific assumptions for the family interactional framework were Waller (1938), Hill (1951), Stryker (1959, 1964), Hill and Hansen (1960), and Haley (1961).

The following comment by Nye and Berardo (1967) provides one description of the linkages between the interactional framework and family theory:

> The interactional framework in sociology and social psychology applied to family study is a framework that has grown crescively. Mead set forth the framework in 1934 and very few attempts have been made at extending or refining his outline. Waller (1938), Waller and Hill (1951), Stryker (1959, 1964), and Hill and Hansen (1960) represent steps in the conceptualization of the approach as applied to the family (Nye and Berardo, 1967, pp. 11-12).

Other theoretical rationale for this study besides the interactional approach, was developed in social psychiatric studies such as The Stirling County Study where the sociocultural factors involved in the origin, course, and outcome of psychiatric disorder were explored. The overarching hypothesis of that study -- "that (social) disintegration fosters psychiatric disorder" (Hughes, et al., 1960) and the fundamental propositions on which that study was theoretically based, e.g., that interference with the basic striving sentiments results in a distortion of the essential psychical condition which produces psychological stress which may foster the development of psychiatric symptoms (Leighton, 1959, pp. 152-154). These propositions from this earlier research have been modified to serve as theoretical under-

6

pinings for this study which hopes to help close yet another gap in understanding the effects of a particular aspect of the social environment, namely
family integration, in its relationship to the development of mental illness.

Definition of Terms

Family Integration: Family units which are markedly integrated will
exhibit high scores in the following family patterns according to the Cavan
Scale for Rating Family Integration and Adaptability: (1) degree of affection;
(2) amount of joint activities of family members; (3) willingness to sacrifice to
attain family objectives; (4) degree of esprit de corp or family pride; (5) degree
to which solidarity is present; and (6) degree of economic interdependence
(Angell, 1936).

Family integration should be viewed as an ideal type concept describing
a continuum-like phenomenon, even when not accompanied by qualifying words
such as "more" and "less" or "lower levels" and "higher levels." When a
family is described as "integrated" it merely means that it is closer to the
imagined absolute or that it scores higher in the operational measures of
family integration than families with lower scores who would then be described
as disintegrated or nonintegrated. The concept is not a static one but rather
measures a balance of over-all trends and countertrends in family interaction.

Also important to recognize in defining family integration is the acknowledgement that family closeness can be noxious as well as benign or beneficial.
Family integration as measured by Cavan's Scale is qualified by definition

to refer to a positive or healthy state of family organization.

Interaction: Interaction is a term used prolifically in the newer descriptions of family dynamics. It is a diffuse concept that refers to a variety of phenomena: physical contacts, cognitive inter-changes, behavior in which roles are created and validated, and affective behavior. Interaction gives rise to interpersonal meanings which the members have for one another (Sussman, 1959, p. 524).

Essential Psychical Condition: The integration of personality is conceived to have at its core a process (or dynamic equilibrium) which has been labeled the essential psychical condition. This is regarded as a range of psychic activities in the direction toward conflict (or blocking of strivings) and away from the conflict (by numerous restorative devices). It can be considered as a state of optimum tension which is always being either reduced, or exceeded and then restored. When the essential psychical condition is put into disequilibrium, disagreeable or stressful feelings come through to consciousness and the personality is vulnerable to developing psychicatric disorder (Leighton, 1959):

> This, of course, is only one of the gateways to such disorder, but it is the one most under the influence of perception and psychological experience, and hence open in a somewhat special way to sociocultural factors. Other sources of malfunction in the personality system may be grouped as hereditary defect and physiological experience (p. 230).

Striving Sentiments: The essential psychical condition is said to depend on a number of essential striving sentiments described in these ten major categories: (1) physical security; (2) expression of love; (3) securing love; (4) sexual satisfaction; (5) the expression of hostility; (6) the securing of recognition; (7) the expression of spontaneity; (8) orientation in terms of one's place in society; (9) membership in a human group; and (10) a sense of being part of a moral order (Hughes, et al., 1960, p. 414).

The disturbance of the striving sentiments may occur if there is interference by the sociocultural environment. Hence, sociocultural situations can be said to foster psychiatric illness if they interfere with the development and functioning of the essential striving sentiments. The word foster is used to indicate a preparation of the ground for some kinds of psychiatric disorder, but without the further assumption that such disorder necessarily follows (Leighton, 1959, p. 157).

Psychological Stress: Psychological stress refers to the internal emotional turmoil within an individual in response to internal threats, fears, guilts, conflicts, and frustrations. It is a broad concept that has little agreement on its exact definition. The definition that was utilized in this study was made by Barrabee and Von Mering: "Stress is an unpleasant emotional tension engendered in an individual when he feels that he is unable to satisfy his needs within his situation of action" (Myers and Roberts, 1959, p. 16). Stress, then, is that disagreeable feeling one experiences when the essential striving sentiments are blocked.

Psychiatric Symptoms: Psychiatric symptoms is a term used to connote degree of mental health or impairment resulting from psychological stress.

Common psychological symptoms of stress include anxiety, loss of control, fears that are diffuse or specific, fatigue, alienation, disorientation, disordered thinking, etc. The index used to measure psychiatric symptoms in this study was the 22-Item Score of Psychiatric Symptoms Indicating Impairment, developed by the Midtown Manhattan Staff. Items chosen for inclusion in the scale were selected as the ones most likely to be used by clients in describing their psychological problems.

Mental health was operationally defined by the 22-Item Index as a measurable continuum ranging from good (low scores) to poor (high scores) (Lagner, 1962, pp. 229-276). In this study designated categories were used to group scores on the 22-Item Index into normal, mildly impaired and severely impaired, as comparative measures of degree of mental health or impairment.

Justification of the Study

The relationship of diverse kinds of family interaction to the mental health of marital pairs is a much discussed but as yet unchartered area. Exploding divorce rates and the proliferation of new family lifestyles have captured the interest of the lay public and drawn the attention of many social and behioral scientists. Still, scientific focus that goes beyond subjective views or value laden descriptions is rare. By analyzing data pertinent to the problem of this study but collected with other primary research goals in mind, this study sought to add some objective findings to help family theorists to answer important questions about how family interaction may produce psychopathology in an individual family member and to help delineate what the essentials are in family life for healthy development. A clearer understanding of the functions of the family and what is requisite in family interaction to enable it to fulfill the mental health needs of the spouses and thus help promote the psychologically healthy development of offspring is sorely needed.

Delimitations of the Study

This study did not purport to be a comprehensive study of family integration or mental health. It was part of a larger sociological study conducted during the fall and winter of 1969 consistent with the principles of survey research. The original study had a two-fold purpose: (1) to find out how psychological social and personal factors affect arthritis, and (2) to ascertain the extent of utilization of medical services in the community. The writer helped to collect data for this original study, and although arthritis or medical utilization were not primary interest of the researcher, several of the indices and measures included in the original questionnaire resulted in the collection of data pertinent to the study of family integration and its association to the mental health heads of households. The advantages of utilizing data already collected are obvious. The disadvantages or limitations imposed on the study are also apparent.

In determining to study the possible psychological effects of low levels of family integration on heads of households, a necessary choice was made to attack just one of the many possible views of the etiology of mental illness--

the interactional. Also, since mental illness has a "multi-dimensional causal pattern" (Meyers and Roberts, 1959, p. 5), it might have been argued that the presence of psychological stress and/or psychiatric symptoms in heads of households could lead to the development of lower levels of integration in their families. Since it would be impossible to study all aspects of the interrelationships between psychiatric disorder and sociocultural factors at the same time, this arbitrary focusing on the potential effects of family environment on the prevalence of psychological stress that may lead to psychiatric symptoms in family heads was recognized as a limitation of the study.

In theoretically designing this study, therefore, level of family integration was chosen as the independent or antecedent variable, and the prevalence of psychiatric symptoms as a reaction to the psychological stress of living in a family with a low score in family integration was considered the dependent or consequent variable.

Other limitations of the study are those obviously inherent due to the complexity of the phenomenon being studied. For example, in psychiatric disorders, as in other fields of medicine, such as tuberculosis, absence of symptoms does not necessarily mean absence of defect (Leighton, 1959, p. 113), and because successful defense mechanisms can result in controlled behavior, a proliferation of symptoms isn't always indicative of disturbed functioning. Add to these, the further complications that people do not pass their whole lives with their families of procreation or of orientation--but

12

are exposed to various other influences in associations, institutions, religious groups or roles, and the complexity of the problem is approximated. The researcher must also contend with the confounding of intervening variables when the noxious effects of conditions related to one of these groups may be neutralized or masked by the benign effects of another (Leighton, 1959, p. 290).

Leighton summed up some of the frustrations of research in the mental health field succinctly when he wrote:

> All this adds up to a formidable state of affairs from the standpoint of research regarding the causal influences of socio-cultural factors. One could well be discouraged by a field in which the various types of cases go about disguised as each other and in which on occasion the seemingly well may be actually more ill than the seemingly sick. The picture is not improved by the realization that we have not even touched on the additional and extraordinarily difficult problems raised by cultural relativity (Leighton, 1959, p. 114).

If researchers remained discouraged by complex tasks, little research would ever be accomplished. Realistically based studies acknowledge that progress in the mental health area as well as understanding in any research problem depends on moving through successive approximations toward an understanding of the relative importance of some causes as compared to others (Leighton and Thomas, 1960, p. 58).

With the foregoing limitations in mind, this study represents a research effort designed to explore just one of the many important pieces in the complex puzzle representing the etiology of mental illness.

Significance of the Study

Hopefully this study will contribute to the accumulating knowledge of family theories and particularly to learnings concerned with the effects of interaction within the family on the mental health of the marital pair. The study was based on the conceptual framework of the interactional approach and therefore was focused on the need to help forward the integration of family dynamics with the understanding of individual intrapsychic dynamics (Meissner, 1964, p. 34).

If it can be demonstrated that a high level of family integration is associated with good mental health for spouses, the study could make practical contributions to family therapists by delineating some of the objective criteria of family integration, for example, those aspects of family interaction measured by Cavan's Scale items. These criteria could then be used to evaluate family functioning. Such a theoretical model could not only facilitate aspects of diagnosis and formulation of a treatment plan, but also be readily conveyed to troubled family members. When a therapist can objectively define potentially noxious or beneficial situations in specific ways, hope for relief is more readily generated.

Also, it is anticipated that through this scrutiny of the more interactional aspects of family life findings will result to help resolve some of the conflicting research views around the issue of the etiology of mental illness. Mathews (1963) called for such a study when he wrote about the "fruitfulness" of a study that would take a sociological rather than a psychological approach to marital and familial happiness. He called for a focus of attention:

> . . . on interaction, on a dynamic and changing relationship; on a dialectical process of responding negatively and positively to what happens during marriage rather than on the static personality traits of the individual (Mathews and Milhanovich, 1963, p. 304).

By focusing on family integration, this study took such a sociological stance. Its purpose was to help build on past research and to add to the growing evidences that point toward the prime importance of interactional factors in the development of psychiatric symptoms. Its findings could help gather evidence to bear on the broad hypothesis that disintegration, within societies or within family units, helps to foster psychiatric disorder. New research understandings generated by this study could have practical value to marriage and family counselors and others who deal with the social problems resulting from family breakdown and mental illness. New findings also could be useful in implementing preventative as well as corrective procedures.

Overview of the Study

The body of this dissertation is divided into three main sections. The first (Chapters I and II) dealt with background materials on theory and research literature in the area of family integration and the implications that various forms of familial lifestyle and marital interaction have for the success or failure of the family as a unit and for the individual family members in terms of mental health. A psychosocial approach to family materials was emphasized.

The second section (Chapter III) described the research procedures followed in this study including discussion of the conceptual model, the hypotheses, the sample, and the operational measures of the variables under study. Chapter IV contained the presentation and analysis of data. Chapter V concentrated on summary, results and recommendations for future research.

CHAPTER II

REVIEW OF LITERATURE

Historical Overview of Family Studies

Despite the frequency with which the human family has been studied there is yet much diversity among theorists and many unresolved issues in family theories. Attempts to synthesize or to integrate existing family materials have been made with varying measures of success, but there is no one theory in the area of the family in which the propositions are lawlike. It has been suggested by Christensen that "for some time at least, family theory is likely to remain middle-ranged and multi-focused" (Christensen, 1964, p. 301).

In the historical development of family study, systematic research was not known before the late 1800's. This was largely because of the taboos attributed to the study of such "private" areas as family life. According to Christensen (1964):

> The development of investigations concerning marriage and the family may be seen as falling into four periods or stages, which can be labeled according to their dominant orientations: (1) pre-research, (2) social Darwinism, (3) emerging science, and (4) systematic theory building (pp. 5-10).

Pre-scientific studies of the family were mostly institutional and historical in perspective. In the late 1800's social Darwinistic explanations were prevalent and explanations of marriage and the family, as with other social institutions, were given in terms of evolution and progress. After the period of social Darwinism, with its emphasis on large-scale comparative studies, came a period of evaluation when the social problems of the family began to emerge as the focal point of studies that were becoming increasingly more empirical (Christensen, 1964, pp. 5-10).

During the twentieth century the tempo and interest in family study has steadily expanded. This change of focus and thrust has been described by Waller (1951):

> It is no longer considered a virtue to be naive or ignorant about the family. We want to learn as much about it as we can and to understand it as thoroughly as possible, for there is a rising recognition in America that vast numbers of its families are sick -- from internal frustrations and from external buffeting. We are engaged in the process of reconstructing our family institutions through criticism and discussion"(p. 4).

The recognition and acknowledgement that families were "sick" and that sick families produced sick people, resulted in studies which combined mental health and family theories in efforts to unravel the secrets of family interaction and to ascertain how the family influenced psychological well being.

The Family as a System

One giant step in understanding family dynamics has been the thrust toward viewing the family as a system. Primary in understanding the family as a social system is the concept that different component parts or members of the family mutually fit and adapt to one another to form a rather rigid patterning of interactions:

18

In a naturalistic situation like the home each person in a situation stimulates the others around him who, in turn, stimulates him. In such an interacting system, there gradually emerges a stable pattern of behavior on the part of all members of the system (Baldwin, 1968, p. 539).

These "stable patterns of behavior" within the family have also been described by Eisenstein (1956), who says that the family molds the kind of persons it needs in order to carry out its functions. Once these roles become established into a working pattern of inter-personal relationships, they are resistant to change and this is one reason why Eisenstein describes the family in terms of a "closed energy system."

In many respects the family relationship resembles what physicists call a "closed energy system." By law and tradition it is one of the most protected relationships existing in civilized society. Indeed, the family is a law unto itself, a microcosmic state within a state (p. 208).

Laws and traditions are not all that protect the familial relationships for there are also built in resistances to change in this social system. The "barricading of family relationships described above leads to a condition of homeostasis or equilibrium" according to Ackerman (1961):

A chief foundation stone for building the understanding of the family as an interactional field is the concept of homeostasis. Ackerman and Jackson, particularly, have illuminated this concept. Borrowed from the physiological sciences, it gives coherent meaning to the intricate pattern of transactional processes in the family. A life force operates in the family through alignments between individuals, joining of identities, complementation, and other processes. This force tends to equilibrate, stabilize, and continuously adapt and readapt family members to each other, and the family to its individuals, in the face of changes from within and from without. Josselyn has termed it a "steering mechanism." Its effect is contripetal and gyroscopic and it is in actuality an adaptational process that maintains family equilibrium (p. 22).

This family homeostasis or equilibrium can be either positive and functional or negative and dysfunctional for the individual member's development.

In viewing the family as a closed energy system with stable patterns of behavior, one can readily see how each family develops an "emotional culture" (Mathew and Mihanovitch, 1963), or an "intra-family environment" (Lidz, 1958) that is uniquely its own. Hess and Handel (1950) refer to this phenomenon of the family's building and inhabiting "its own emotional life-space," in their book Family Worlds:

> There is a sense in which a family is a bounded universe. The members of a family -- parents and their young children -- inhabit a world of their own making, a community of feeling and fantasy, action and precept (p. 99).

In addition to building a world of its own, each family develops basic patterns of relating to the external world and also of managing interpersonal involvements through what Hess and Handel (1950) call the "family theme," which he described as:

> . . . a pattern of feelings, motives, fantasies, and conventionalized understandings grouped about some locus of concern which has a particular form in the personalities of the individual members. The pattern comprises some fundamental view of reality and some way or ways for dealing with it. In the family themes are to be found the family's implicit directions, its notions of "who we are" and "what we do about it" (p. 11).

Thus, the intermeshing of familial multiple relationships creates a family structure that has a meaning over and above the meaning of its parts (Sussman, 1959, p. 521). Just as each family system is unique in its complexity, it is also unique in the individualized meaning that it will have for each of its members.

The sociologist and the interactionist view the family as an interdependent system of individuals operating within the norms of a given society (Baldwin, 1968). Seeing the family as a system and as a group requires analyses and descriptions that deal with small group dynamics and conceptual frameworks that explicate the processes of interaction among group members. Students of the intrafamilial environment are indebted to pioneer sociologists like Burgess, Parsons, and Bales and their co-workers, J. Speigel and F. Kluckhohn, Nathan Ackerman, Bradley Buell and the Community Research Associates and many others for their efforts in analyzing marital and family inter-relationships (Lidz, 1957, p. 242). The base they have provided is the foundation on which family researchers have built and seek to build yet more complete theory.

Effects of Family Socialization

Socialization not only begins in the family, but it is also considered one of the major functions of family interaction (Vernon, 1964, p. 335). Although there are many levels of socialization, from the cognitive to the affective, and it is evident that various institutions within society provide the predominant source of socialization at different periods within an individual's lifetime, the family is considered the original social matrix (Clausen, 1956, p. 135) and most studies of socialization concentrate upon childhood training

(Shibutani, 1961, p. 479).

In his recent article on "Schizophrenia and the Family,"
Theodore Lidz recognizes that while the family is not the only
influence upon personality development, it provides what he terms
"the most consistent--or consistently inconsistent--set of influences
impinging upon the maturing child" (Hatch and Hatch, 1962, p. 213).

In sociological terms, socialization has been defined as the process
by which individuals acquire the knowledge, skills, and dispositions that enable
them to participate as more or less effective members of groups and the society
(Brimm, 1966). The more specific aims of socialization have been described by
Broom and Selznick (1955, p. 87) as: (1) the inculcation of basic disciplines,
(2) instilling of aspirations or ideals, (3) teaching of social roles and their
supporting attitudes, and (4) the teaching of skills.

It has been a major discovery of psychoanalysis that ways of thinking
and patterns of relating with other people that are programed or socialized
earliest in life are often programed hardest. People tend to repeat "compul-
sively" all of their lives' forms of relating that were prefigured in infancy
(Schatzman, 1973, pp. 25-26). This idea of the rigidity of temperamental
traits and their configuration as being fixed in the earliest years of childhood
into "invariable reactive systems" as the result of emotional aspects of family
interaction has also been conceptualized by Sapir and named "the psychiatric
personality" (Cavan and Ranck, 1971, p. x) . Thus there is much theory to
support the paramount importance that socialization within the family can
have upon the psychological health of its members.

However, in analyzing the complex reasons why people behave as they do, more factors than merely childhood socialization and conditioning

within the family need to be taken into account. For instance, Hess and

Handel (1959) pointed out:

> Recognizing that each infant possesses an irreducible
> psychobiological individuality that no amount or kind of
> intense socialization can abolish, the dual condition of
> inevitable individuality and unescapable psychosocial con-
> nection remains and is a dynamic condition that is a basic
> social fact for family theory to consider (pp. 4-5).

> Case histories are replete with accounts of children
> who have been psychologically marred by interaction with
> disturbed parents, but also, cases occasionally emerge to
> illustrate the possibility that children may resist contagion
> and react to pathology with health (p. 147).

Also relevant to understanding this complex relationship between

environment and personality development is the fact that people are

involved in their families in very different ways (Hess and Handel, 1959,

pp. 99-100), and in order to understand why such differential effects on

individual members are possible within the same family system, one would

also have to have some basis on which to evaluate the importance of the

family for a specific member's emotional economy.

In commenting on this difficulty of assessing the effects of articula-

tion between the individual and his family system, Ackerman (1958) made

this astute observation:

> None of us lives his life alone. Those who try are fore-
> doomed; they disintegrate as human beings (p. 15).

However, Ackerman then went on to point out that some individuals

who live with their families are also foredoomed to disintegrate as human beings by becoming victims of mental illnesses of varying kinds and degrees through the channels of interfamilial interaction, psychic contagion and a process of socialization which is pathological in its effects on family members:

> Some aspects of life experience are, to be sure, more individual than social, others more social than individual; but life is nonetheless a shared and a sharing experience. In the early years this sharing occurs almost exclusively with members of our family. The family is the basic unit of growth and experience, fulfillment or failure. It is also the basic unit of illness and health (Ackerman, 1958, p. 15).

As the "basic unit of illness and health" the family as a system of interdependent and dynamically interacting parts is increasingly becoming the focal point in research aimed at uncovering the variables related to the development of mental illness. Recognized as important in these inquiries is the fact that "the intrapsychic organization of each member is part of the psychosocial structure of his family (Hess and Handel, 1950, p. 3).

Various systems of explanation for maladaptive personal adjustment other than through socialization have been outlined. One such attempt by Mechanic (1969) included the perspectives of learning theory, social-stress, societal reaction in addition to the psychosocial-developmental approach. Explanations of mental illness that are solely physiological or hereditary have their exponents, and research seems to indicate that there is "as much basis for the hereditary theory as there is for any other" (Mechanic, 1969, p. 35).

However, family research that is interactionist based is more and more turning to the interactional approach and to the psychosocial interior of the family in efforts to demonstrate how the mental health of family members is interrelated. This emphasis is concerned with the multiple interpersonal factors that act as distorting influences upon personality—with "development rather than cause" (Lidz, 1958, p. 515).

From his theoretical stance comes such vocabulary as "psychic contagion," "induced insanity," and "the psychosis of association." The transference of delusional ideas and/or abnormal behavior from one adult person to another who is in close association is also stressed (Prims, 1950, pp. 324, 338).

In the forefront of investigators into "distortions of mentation," "paralogical thinking," and "training in irrationality" that occurs within the family as "a primary teacher of social interaction and emotional reactivity" are Lidz and his associates who stated that:

> The family forms the first imprint upon the still unformed child and is the most pervasive and consistent influence that establishes patterns that later forces can modify but never alter completely (Lidz, et al., 1963, p. 20).

Lidz's studies of schizophrenic families have led him to conclude that the ability to live in such a family would require "special, devious and even bizarre strategies" from its members, and concluded, "the irrationality of the schizophrenic finds its rationality in the context of his first family;" and that the schizophrenic's conceptual disorders "do not rise de novo out of their own life problems, but have precursors in the perception and thinking of the parents who raised them and provided most of their early education in problem solving and linguistic usage" (Lidz, 1963, pp. 100, 159).

Henry (1971) described in an almost poetic way the process of "consciousness making" and the large area of unknown as to "the way the average parent's needs shape the child" (p. 59) in his book Pathways to Madness:

> For such empathic absorption of the universe by the baby it is probably better to use the word "imbue" rather than "teach." When one is imbued in this way--as if the sun, water and time were filtered to one through the body of another person--it becomes difficult to change one's perceptions, for change would be a kind of death--a detachment from the person through whom the universe was absorbed. Thus consciousness itself is learned and acquired through another person. From the time we are born we are taught HOW TO BE CONSCIOUS (p. 60).

Being given a unique and perhaps distorted brand of consciousness through socialization in a disturbed family can place the individual in the position of possessing "unshared" and "unsharable" ways of experiencing the world. This kind of faulty socialization seems to Lidz (1958) to help explain some kinds of schizophrenic adaptations:

> A theory of schizophrenia must explain not only the patient's needs to abandon reality testing but also his ability to do so, and why some persons can escape through withdrawal into unshared ways of experiencing the world around them more readily than others (p. 306).

Being raised amidst a "folie a famille" -- where the entire family shares aberrant conceptualization (Lidz, 1958, p. 246) can produce other problems less dramatic than schizophrenia. Seeing all mental illness on

26

a continuum, it is possible to generalize from the studies more specifically concerned with the interactional nature and development of paralogical thinking in schizophrenic families to the understanding of the processes involved in the transmission of ideas, beliefs, attitudes, and ways of communicating and relating that can prove problematical or as blocks to the achievement of a positive mental health. For instance, role dysfunctions learned within a troubled family constellation can have far-reaching negative effects on the mental health of individual family members. Glasser and Glasser (1970) submitted the following:

> For the individual affiliated with highly idiosyncratic role definitions as a result of dysfunction within the family of origin, the probability of establishing satisfying reciprocities in the family of procreation is reduced. This will lead to lowered self-evaluation, and thus to intrapsychic distress with its vicissitudes. Thus is role dysfunction transmuted into psychopathology (p. 161).

For the student of the family, finding myriads of pieces of research evidence to support the thesis of transmission of mental illness through the auspices of family interaction is easy. The researcher soon begins to form doubts, however, about the myth of "normality" as it applies to mental health, and to become down right cynical with regard to narratives of romance and marriage that equate stability in marriage with happiness in marriage.

The Myth of Normality

"Normal" is often seen more discreetly than is warranted. The spectrum is wide and the variability almost infinite within the normal. Many families that do not have hospitalized members nevertheless have ways of interacting and patterns of expectation and belief which, under the scrutiny of family therapists would probably be seen as unhealthy or restrictive to individual development. It is no secret, although certainly neither a publicized fact, that the hospitalized portion of the world's population represents only the top of the iceberg of mental illness. Borderline and ambulatory cases in various diagnostic categories abound and are abroad in the land as family members and family heads of households. Pathology is spread from one generation to another, undetected and uncorrected, since it has not reached sufficient proportions to justify therapeutic intervention or diagnostic labels. One wonders how much of the incidence of mental illness and problematic relating in families can be traced to families in trouble that are seen as "normal."

In some dysfunctional families one would be hard-pressed to pinpoint the most "abnormal" member since often the "illest" person is not the one to act out his pathology in symptomatic ways that are socially defined as "sick." Unless the family's pain is such that society at large is affected or disrupted in some way, the sick family with a sick member is often seen to be "normal" rather than a system that is producing symptoms of its pain in one acting out member. Virginia Satir (1964) concluded that a symptom in one family member represents an expression of dysfunction in the entire family, and that family pain is the reason for, not the result of, the individual member's symptoms. This phenomenon was explained beautifully by the concept of the "identified patient":

> Family therapists deal with family pain. When one person
> in a family (the "identified patient") has pain which shows up in
> symptoms, all family members are feeling this pain in some
> way. The therapist sees the identified patient's symptoms as
> serving a family function as well as an individual function (p. 1).

Well integrated, close knit families have often been viewed as "healthy"

across the board, and little distinction has been made between families that

are close in a healthy way and families that are cemented together in fear

and/or mentally ill ways. Only more recently has the literature in the

family area reflected the realization that there are different kinds of close-

ness and family integration. Cavan's scale sought to measure positive aspects

of family solidarity. Jordan (1972) has made some beginning attempts to

develop a typology for describing families in terms that acknowledge differ-

ences in family organization. Jordan wrote about families that tended to draw

its members inward and families that thrust its members outside the family

sphere. The two categories suggested were integrative and centrifugal:

> The origins of both emotional patterns lie in a conflict
> between those needs and aspirations which draw family members
> together for mutual help and support and the needs and aspirations
> which drive individual members into the outside world (p. 27).

In the integrative family the emotional needs of the parents are too

strong. They don't let their children go, and try instead to create their own

self-sufficient social system within the family circle. When there is trouble,

this kind of family tends to draw together and tries to bury its differences.

To the centrifugal family the emotional content in the family's life is habitually denied or played down, and family members seek to satisfy all their emotional needs in social activities away from the home. When this kind of family is faced with trouble, solutions are sought outside the family and usually seen in terms of the environmental or material (Jordan, 1972, p. 40).

In making the observation that both types of families have some strengths as well as some considerable weaknesses, Jordan forces the acknowledgment that close family integration is not always analogous to family strength or health and indeed shakes the myth so prevalent in early literature and in some writings today that equate close family integration with health or normalcy without first discovering or delimiting the criteria that form the basis for the closeness.

With respect to the "normalcy" or "pathogenic" quality to be found in specific families, Henry (1971) commented after having lived as a participant observer in several families that had produced psychotic members:

> . . . yet none of us is free of the kinds of problems they have, nor entirely free of their defects, and I have tried to make that clear (p. xv).

The myth of the normal family that produces mentally healthy offspring just because it is close or well integrated without first defining the source of that closeness is not unlike the myth that a "stable" marriage reflects a healthy marital relationship and produces children less apt to be mentally ill.

The Myth of "Togetherness Equals Happiness"

Much of the research of the sixties had to do with the development of

testing devices to measure marital stability, marital satisfaction, marital

happiness, marital success, or marital adjustment (Hicks and Platt, 1970).

The prevailing attitude guiding this research seemed to be that marital happi-

ness or success and marital stability and adjustment were synonymous kinds

of terms. However, some disquieting findings began to emerge to disturb

such research assumptions. It was discovered that divorce wasn't always a

good measure of marital satisfaction since some couples felt it necessary to

"stick it out" in the marriage whether they were satisfied or not (Kieren and

Tollman, 1972, p. 247). Also, other data began to suggest that stability

might not be as dependent upon marital happiness as had been assumed

(Hicks and Platt, 1970, p. 562).

> Current data indicate clearly that the factors which make
> a marriage brittle or durable are infinitely more complicated
> than just "being happy" (Hicks and Platt, 1970, p. 569).

> Cuber and Harroff (1963) found that stable marriages are
> not necessarily stable because they are deeply satisfying. A stable
> pair may on the one hand be deeply fulfilled people, living vibrantly,
> or at the other extreme entrapped, embittered, resentful people,
> living lives of duplicity in an atmosphere of hatred and despair
> (Hicks and Platt, 1970, p. 141).

The "empty-shell" marriage was acknowledged and described by

Goode (1969) as one:

> . . . in which people carry out their formal duties toward
> one another, but give no understanding, affection, or support,
> and have little interest in communicating with one another (p. 100).

With such data to contend with the problem of determining what made marriages last became more complicated. The recognition that neurotic interaction and/or unconscious collusion between the marital pair could be the basis for a marriage that might be complementary and thus stable, while at the same time being neurotic making or pathogenic for the couple and their offspring, led researchers into new areas of inquiry. Along with acknowledging that sometimes it was the unhappy marriages that were "stable," the "fit of the family" or of the marital relationship began to be discussed and classified, e.g., neurotic or rhythmic (Shostrum and Kavanaugh, 1971). Sometimes "neurotic" fits were even defended as not always "bad" or unhealthy as a basis for a family's integration. Younghusband (1967) wrote:

> Neurotic symptoms, oddities, and unconventional role assignments need not necessarily lead to unhappy families or severely maladjusted children as long as the members of the family can play roles which help to fulfill their own as well as the needs of others in the family and as long as there is some capacity to tolerate individual differences and some sharing of common values. Only when emotional instability is combined with incompatability between the parents and conflicting values, does the family cohesion and the mental health of their members seem seriously threatened (p. 26).

Other researchers, however, defended the thesis that unhealthy or neurotic adjustments in families eventually take a toll on both the marital pair and the children of such a union. LeMasters (1969) made a study of couples who had lived in troubled marriages for at least ten years and discovered that seventy-eight percent had suffered some personal disorganization as a result of maintaining a "stable" but stressful marriage. He concluded that these couples who were joined in "holy deadlock" did not "escape the destructive impact of marital failure by avoiding separation or divorce" (p. 435).

Renne's findings seem to corroborate LeMasters' theory of personal disorganization within a stressful or unhappy marriage. He wrote:

> Data seem to justify an analogy between unhappy marriage and disability. The disability imposed by an unsatisfactory marriage is analogous to the disability imposed by minority race, chronic illness, economic deprivation, or a missing limb (p. 348).

Renne's (1970) findings indicated that unhappily married people were more likely to have physical and/or mental health problems than were either divorced or happily married people of the same race, sex and age (p. 338), and he therefore concluded:

> For this disability (unhappy marriage), divorce is probably the most effective remedy (p. 6).

Researchers also have explored whether or not the impact of an unhappy marriage may have a different effect on men and women.

Both Laws (1971) and Gove (1972) reported a differential impact of an unhappy marriage on the two sexes; with women seemingly suffering more psychological damage than men. Laws said, "a case could be made that marriage is not good for women," (Laws, 1971, p. 510) and Gove concluded that since married women had more mental illness than other women who were divorced, widowed or single, that this increased rate of mental illness could be "attributed to the role of the married woman," (Gove, 1972, p. 34).

Henry (1971) agreed that the effects of adult socialization within marriage could be important clues in understanding mental health since at any point in life a person might encounter situations that could have pathogenic effects. He posed a provocative question in forwarding his contention that "people drive people mad," when he asked:

> Since under proper environmental conditions a psychotic adult may be restored to sanity, why isn't it likely that under improper environmental conditions he may lose his sanity (p. 373).

Such questions surely must be part of the new reality of family research if it is to move beyond myths of "normal" families and like myths that stable marriages are happy or that marriages can be divided into either healthy or neurotic categories. Research and experience force the acknowledgment that all marital partners complement each other's more neurotic as well as less neurotic qualities (Josselyn, 1953, p. 156) and pushes family theorists to formulate new descriptions and typologies for marriage and the family that related to reality rather than fantasy--to facts rather than to our hopes and needs.

Macrosocial Effects on the Family

In recent literature in addition to attention to the effects of "domestic" or interior affairs upon mental health in the family, a new emphasis has been placed upon "foreign affairs" or macrosocial influences upon the family. The necessity of having a "fit" between family values and ways of living and those of the larger social group or network in which the family is embedded (Younghusband, 1967, p. 27) has received research focus. Hence, the "Happily ever after" myth for families has been pushed to recognize twin dangers--the micro reality that a family often includes one or more cruel or pathogenic people--and the macro reality that social situations often impinge in family happiness by requiring renunciation of personal desires (Josselyn, 1957, p. 331).

The impact of the larger culture of which the family is a part has been increasingly recognized by social scientists in their efforts to assess the broader social and cultural factors that affect mental health. Becker and Hill (1948), Wallter and Hill (1951), Nye (1957), Parad and Caplan (1960), Lidz (1963), Winch (1971), Laws (1971), Henry (1971), Jordan (1972), and Skolnick (1973) all have stressed the necessity of taking into account the environmental, economic, and cultural factors that impinge upon the family and influence its development as a system as well as the well being and con- sciousness of its members. This macrosocial view sees family not as an isolated entity, but as a functioning social system interrelated with other social systems in society (Cavan, 1969, p. 365).

With regard to the effects that economic aspects of the macro culture can have on families, some family researchers point out that socio-economic status can have an impact on the relationships within the family. In com- menting on some of the factors that place stress on the family, Glasser and Glasser (1970) reported:

Interpersonal attraction can only be maintained in the context of an adequate and stable income. Love, respect, and self-actualization can only become goals in a marriage after subsistence and safety have been achieved (p. 92).

Other researchers have noted the increase in both divorce and mental illness with decreasing social class (Blumenthal, 1967, p. 605) and it remains for future researchers to determine whether this negative impact is a result of income alone or in conjunction with lower levels of education or some other intervening variable or variables.

When considering family life and its impact upon mental health, it is quite disconcerting to read assertions that "eighty to ninety percent of the population show up as starkly emotionally disordered" (Charny, 1972, p. 72). Such a statement leads to a curiosity about the various weights of intra personal, interpersonal, and supra personal factors upon the mental health of individuals (Parad and Caplan, 1960, p. 3) and the necessity for making further inquiries into the part each plays in the development of neurosis and other mental illness.

In other recent literature the importance of recognizing and research-ing the current macrosocial movements or "revolutions" of our day "in the culture at large" is mentioned. Carl Rogers' (1972) latest book <u>Becoming Partners: Marriage and Its Alternatives</u>, reflects the trend in society toward more liberal attitudes toward alternative family forms and various non-traditional kinds of relationships. Other researchers are also collecting data to assess what effect the "sexual revolution" will have on the family units within society.

Another macrosocial revolution--the feminist movement--is sure to make its mark upon family life. The implications of this phenomenon on the family and for the mental health of its members has already been marked as necessitating future research focus (Laws, 1971, p. 483).

Overload

Another large general area of concern mentioned in the literature dealing with marriage and the family and the mental health therein is the growing emphasis on the "mental hygiene" function of the family (Mathews and Mihanovitch, 1963, p. 304). Much has been written about the fact that in terms of the functions traditionally seen as being within the pervue of the family, which are: (1) reproduction of population, (2) protection and care of the child, (3) economic production of family goods and services, (4) socialization of the child, (5) education of the child, (6) recreation, (7) affectional interaction (Becker and Hill, 1948, p. 47), that emphasis in the modern, urban nuclear family is more and more being placed on the inter- actional or affective sector. This trend has been described by Burgess and Locke in the phrase "companionship family" (Glasser and Glasser, 1970, p. 337) and Miller and Swanson allude to the same phenomenon in their term "colleague family" (Miller and Swanson, 1958, pp. 198-207). Farber (1964) also recognized this trend when he wrote of the family as becoming more and more a mediating or emotional support system by presenting its "permanent- availability" quality as a main source of its strength and function for family members. In 1963, Goode described the growing importance of the family's task of restoring the "input-output emotional balance" of its members, and Parsons and Bales (1955) stated that the "basic and irreducible functions" of the modern American family are (a) the socialization of children so they can become members of the society in which they are born, and (b) the stabilization of the adult personalities of the population of the society (pp. 16-17).

Predictions for life in the future include more leisure time and shortened work weeks. This, coupled with possibilities of fuel and energy shortages, will mean that families will be faced with both "more togetherness and more apartness and an important change in family life will be that the bonds are affectional rather than functional" (Farson, 1969, p. 63).

This stressing of the family as the primary source for "the giving and receiving of love" and the home as the place where "social relations are most easily seen in the raw" (Waller, 1951, p. 34) may lead to an "overload" with which the family of the future may not be able to cope. Farson (1969) warned:

> As a reaction against the supernatural, supertechnical world, people will allow themselves to be more irrational and more infantile within the family. We shall see this happening in the family because it is about the only setting in which it can happen. There will be few places in the world of the future in which we can find privacy or a safe place for expressing aggressive and hostile impulses. So family life will be highly emotional, intimate, infantile, aggressive, hostile, and irrational (p. 59).

This kind of colliding of family members behind closed doors (Waller, 1938, p. 26) was also described in a quote by Filman in Perutz's

38

(1972) book, <u>Marriage Is Hell</u>:

> The first tendency of the incessant home life is to exaggerate personality. The home is necessarily a hot bed of personal feeling. There love grows intense and often morbid; there any little irritation frets and wears in the constant pressure like a stone in one's shoe (p. 183).

Aside from the issue of "overloading" the family's coping mechanisms with such heavy emotional duties, there is also the problem of unrealistic expectations. Winch (1966) had this comment to make on the unrealistic expectations of family life that are fostered along other American dreams:

> The American culture, it seems fosters the expectation that life is and should be orderly and that families, like new automobiles, should run quietly and smoothly. Just as reflection brings the realization that jalopies, too, are part of our system of transportation, so it is important to realize that disorder is generally as natural as order, disease as natural as health, and that familial disorganization is not a recently spawned evil of the atomic age (p. 689).

Another factor compounding problems of unrealistic expectations of family life is relative deprivation. Farson (1969) made a sage commentary regarding the kind of relative deprivation that occurs because people in the 1970's are generally expecting more from marriage and family life than they ever have before:

> And so really the frustration and discontent in family life arises from the discrepancy between what one has and what one sees it is possible to have. FRUSTRATIONS ARISE, ESSENTIALLY, FROM THE IMPROVEMENT IN FAMILY LIFE. For the great paradox about any improvement is this: instead of giving satisfaction and contentment, improvements simply bring increased discontent and the need for more improvement. We know that revolutions follow reform rather than precede it. In history this has been the case quite uniformly. We have seen this most clearly in the civil rights movement.

So that is the problem in marriage. Marriage is a failure only in relation to something. The question is this: compared to what is it a failure? It is a failure compared to the excitement that can be generated by extramarital affairs. And it is a failure compared to the idealized picture that is held up to us in the mass media. It is a failure compared to the fantasies we have about other "happy" couples. And it is a failure compare to our expectations of what it might be. But marriage is not a failure compared to what it used to be (pp. 64-66).

Summary

Marriage and family life may be as Farson suggests, better than ever, but paradoxically there is more awareness of families in crisis, and more complaints are made by family members about physical abuse, verbal abuse, financial problems, excessive drinking, neglect of the home and children, mental cruelty, in-law trouble, excessive demands, infidelity, sexual incompatibility, and lack of love (Glasser and Glasser, 1970, p. 129). Along with the loss of reticence on the part of family members to report negatives about their families, the temerity of social scientists to dissect and scrutinize family processes is also gone:

Fifty years or more ago, most people had the greatest respect for the institution called the family and wished to learn nothing whatever about it. Their phrases remain with us today: "No nation is stronger than its homes." "A man's home is his castle." "The family is the cornerstone of the society and the bulwark of civilization." Those statements were even then empty cliches, which carried little weight in the formation of national policies or in local community planning. Our society has taken the family for granted, ignored it, shunted it aside, and expected it to do the nation's patching and mending without regard or attention.

Today much of that has been changed. Gone is the conceal-
ment of the way in which life begins, gone the irrational sanctity
of the home. The aura of sentiment which once protected the
family from discussion clings to it no more. It is no longer considered a virtue to be naive or ignorant about the family. We want
to learn as much about it as we can and to understand it as thoroughly
as possible for there is a raising recognition in America that vast
numbers of its families are sick--from internal frustrations and
from external buffeting. We are engaged in the process of recon-
structing our family institutions through criticism and discussion
(Waller, 1951, pp. 3-4).

Even as current literature reflects the belief in looking more deeply

into the family as a psychological unit and also broadens out to explore

cultural diversities and the macrosocial changes of a modern day society,

we are reminded that there are some basic components of family life and of

relationships that do not change.

In forming our concept of the nature of the family, we must
not be led astray by the diversity of family forms. We must
not forget the endless variety of form or the infinite spawning of
customs, but neither must we overvalue them. Above all, we
must not fail to see that there are certain aspects of family
life which are much the same in all times and places.

Times change, and we change with them, and human nature
changes too, but the more it changes, the more some parts of it
remain the same. Our book, is focused directly upon these relatively stable aspects of the family, upon the attitudes generated
by the impact of one person upon another in the process of living
together (Waller and Hill, 1951, p. 11).

It is with these universal elements of family life -- "the impact of

one person upon the other in the process of living together" -- that this study

has concentrated. It has been an effort to help unravel the interactional

factors of family life which cause subtle but brutal damage to the minds of

those who live therein.

Basic Theoretical Assumptions of the Study

The general theoretical base of this study has been drawn from the theory and research literature of family interaction and social psychiatry. The theory and research propositions utilized in the Stirling County Studies (Leighton, 1959, pp. 152-154) have been modified and augmented to serve as the specific theoretical base from which the research hypotheses of this study have been developed. These assumptions are:

1. All human beings exist in a state of psychological striving.

2. Striving plays a part in the maintenance of an essential psychical condition.

3. Interference with striving leads to a disturbance of the essential psychical condition.

4. Disturbance of the essential psychical condition gives rise to disagreeable feelings -- stress.

5. Given a disturbance of the essential psychical condition, pre-existing defect in personality may contribute toward the development of psychiatric disorder.

6. It seems exceedingly probable that persons living in poorly integrated families will have proportionately greater difficulty in the maintenance of their essential striving sentiments, particularly those concerned with love, recognition, and belonging.

7. The psycho-social environment within a family with low levels

of family integration is such that it may prove disturbing to the essential

psychical condition of its members and give rise to a psychological stress

that may foster the development of psychiatric symptoms.

Hypothesis of the Study

Given the foregoing theoretical rationale one would expect to find that

ongoing socialization in adulthood within the marital relationship, as within

the interactional system of the family of procreation, could have a measur-

able negative or positive impact on the mental health of spouses depending

upon the perceived quality of such relationships and interactions. For

purposes of research on the basic question which this study addressed,

i.e., what effect does family integration have upon the psychological health

of the heads of households, the following hypotheses have been derived from

family theories, research and literature for testing.

1. Persons living in families with lower scores in family integration

will have significantly more psychological stress and psychiatric symptoms

than those persons who live in families with a higher level of family inte-

gration.

2. Controlling for marital status, persons living with a spouse and

having lower scores in family integration will have significantly more

psychiatric symptoms than persons who are divorced, widowed or married

but separated.

3. Women with low scores in family integration will have significantly more psychological stress and psychiatric symptoms than will men with low scores in family integration.

4. Level of family integration will still be predictive of psychiatric symptoms when other social and demographical variables analyzed are held constant.

CHAPTER III

METHODOLOGY

Research Design

This study was conducted in collaboration with a larger sociological study undertaken during the fall and winter of 1969. The original study had a two-fold purpose: (1) to find out how psychological, social and personal factors affect arthritis, and (2) to ascertain the extent of utilization of medical services in the community. The study was under the direction of the Division of Behavioral Science in the Department of Preventive Medicine and the Arthritis Division of the University of Utah Medical Center. It was financed by federal funds from the United States Public Health Service, Department of Health, Education and Welfare.

The methodology of the study was consistent with the principles of the survey research approach: (1) the problem was formulated then placed within the context of a larger body of theory and research; (2) techniques were devised from the collection of data; (3) the sample was selected; (4) the data was collected, and (5) the data was analyzed (Sellitz, Jahoda, Deutch, and Cook, 1964, pp. 65-78).

Sample

As part of the research design, a two-stage stratified systematic random sample of Salt Lake City's 62,000 dwelling units was made. The sampling procedure consisted of (1) stratifying the city's forty-nine census tracts into high and low socioeconomic segments; (2) drawing a predetermined number of blocks at random from each socioeconomic segment with probabilities proportionate to block size; and (3) selecting four household units from each block using a systematic sample based on a random start and a predetermined interval for each block. Names and exact addresses were obtained from a city directory as part of the systematic selection of the household. A household was designated as that person or group of people, related or not, who lived in a dwelling unit, the latter defined as structurally separate living quarters.

The person interviewed in each housing unit was systematically alternated between male and female head of household where a choice was necessary. This was done to reduce the number of unemployed males and housewives in the sample, and resulted in a total N comprised of 208 men and 370 women. Twenty housing units were found to be unoccupied at the time of the attempted interviews. Of the chosen 600 housing units which were found to be occupied, eighty-two percent of the interviews were successfully completed to give a sample number of 578.

With data utilizing the Cavan Family Integration Scale, the total sample number is cut from 578 to 367. The 209 missing observations (36 percent) represented the number of single respondents who did not complete that scale. Two respondents who were single answered the scale but were not utilized in data analysis.

According to the 1970 census, Salt Lake City had the following social demographic characteristics: a total population of 175,798, with 30 percent under age 18; 6 percent foreign born with 14 percent having one parent of foreign extraction, 96 percent were classified as Caucasian with no break-down given for the 4 percent minority population. Fifty-one percent reported membership in the Church of Jesus Christ of Latter-day Saints, for persons over 14; 63 percent of the males and 56 percent of the females were married; family size within the city limits was two and seven-tenths persons per household and the median educational level for persons 25 years of age and older was twelve and one-half years of formalized schooling with 65 percent having at least a high school diploma.

The demographic characteristics of the sample used in this study are proportional to those of the population of Salt Lake, as reflected in the 1970 census data, for most variables. Median education for the sample was twelve and one-tenth years as compared to a city-wide census figure of twelve and five-tenths years. Racially, the 96 percent white proportionate of the sample is almost identical to the city figures. Concerning age, the study did not sample any persons under 16 years of age but does have some 17 percent of its respondents in the 65 and over category, as compared to some 13 percent for the city as a whole. As for marital status, some 62 percent of the sample are married which is close to the city-wide census figures showing 59 percent of Salt Lake's residents to be married. (Although, it must be noted that the census data are based on all persons 14 and over while the sample figures include only persons 16 and over.) One area where the city-wide census figures and sample figures are disproportionate is in regard to religious affiliation, where the respective percentage of Mormons are 51 for the former and 68 for the latter.

Questionnaire

The questionnaire instrument used in the research consisted of a series of standardized scales as well as direct and indirect questions designed to gather data on descriptive information, medical utilization, childhood background and to measure many of the current major concepts used in sociology, social psychology and medical sociology, such as: stress, alienation, anomie, authoritarianism, marital adjustment, family integration, social participation, psychiatric impairment, depression, self-esteem, cosmopolitan-parochialism, social mobility, status inconsistency, adoption of sick role, cultural deprivation, job satisfaction, marriage roles, and a host of others. The scales used in this questionnaire were chosen because they were most frequently used indexes for measuring the above concepts.

The vast amount of information on diverse subjects obtained from such a composite questionnaire made the data thus collected a rich resource for studies other than the original project. Utilizing the data on family integration and psychiatric symptoms collected in research not specifically aimed at studying those variables makes that data even more valuable and more likely to be free from possible reactive or obtrusive research biases.

Data Collection Procedure

The method for data collection was by personal interview. One structured interview lasting approximately one hour was conducted with each respondent utilizing the study's questionnaire. The interviews were administered by a team of interviewers who had advanced training in sociology and who had completed training sessions designed to acquaint them with over-all research procedures and goals specialized interviewing techniques and other procedures aimed at increasing the standardization of the data collection process.

Each interviewer carried a mimeographed letter and a plastic enclosed I.D. card identifying him or her as a professional person and explaining the significance of the research project to the intended respondent. The cooperation of the head of household was requested and an explanation provided as to why that particular residence had been chosen. The majority of respondents were found to be cooperative and interested in being a part of a research endeavor. Each interviewer also kept a journal wherein dates of first contact, call-backs and completions or refusal of interviews was recorded for each residence chosen in the sample.

During the months that the interviews were being conducted in the community, the research director maintained a control desk at the University of Utah Medical Center in order to answer any questions respondents had with regard to the survey, and also to provide a constant resource for the interviewers. Following the completion of the interviewing of the sample, the questionnaires were checked for completeness and accuracy and coded for the computer.

Operational Measures of Family Integration

The variable of family integration has been referred to in the literature by several terms, such as, family solidarity, family unity and family coherence. In some research the terms family integration and marital adjustment have been used interchangeably.

Cavan's Scale for Rating Family Integration and Adaptability: The scale used to measure the concept of family integration in this study was Ruth Shonle Cavan's Scale for Rating Family Integration and Adaptability. This original Cavan scale with six items was developed for use in Angell's classic study, The Family Encounters the Depression, which was published in 1936. Cavan and Ranck used the scale in a follow-up study, The Family and the Depression in 1938, and the scale became the basis for later marital adjustment scales developed by other researchers. For instance, the Burgess and Cottrell Marital Adjustment Test contained many items that were similar to those used in the earlier Cavan scale (Bonjean, 1967, p. 209).

Cavan's scale was more recently used by Hill in his 1949 study of

Families Under Stress. Hill modified the original Cavan scale slightly for

his study to include just five items, one each measuring (1) degrees of

affections, (2) amount of joint activities of family members, (3) willingness

to sacrifice to attain family objectives, (4) degree of esprit de corps or

family pride and (5) degree to which solidarity is present (Jansen, 1952, p.

728). The sixth item of the original scale having to do with economic inter-

dependence was omitted in Hill's study. The Cavan scale was also used by

Jansen in 1952 in his study to measure family solidarity (Jansen, 1952, p.

728).

Cavan's original Scale for Rating Family Integration and Adaptability

was used in this study. An example question for this scale is shown below:

_____ 1. Indicate the amount of affection shared between your
spouse and yourself. (1) Very hostile and tense relationship, (2) minor disagreements and aloofness, (3)
"average," congenial and loyal, (4) in love more than
average, (5) extremely affectionate.

Respondents' answers by number were placed in the left hand space

by each question. The total family integration score was found by adding

up the scores from ten questions which covered the six scale items: (1)

degree of affection; (2) joint activities; (3) mutual cooperation; (4) esprit

de corps; (5) solidarity (as measured by degree of tension present); and

(6) economic interdependence.

For purposes of this study scores on the Cavan Scale were split at

the median to divide the scores into categories representing low family integration and high family integration. The lowest scores through 27 were assigned to category one (low family integration), and the scores from 28 up to the highest to category two (high family integration).

Operational Measure for Psychological
Stress/Mental Health

The 22-Item Score of Psychiatric Symptoms Indicating Impairment: The index used to measure psychiatric symptoms in this study was the 22-Item Score of Psychiatric Symptoms Indicating Impairment developed by the Midtown Manhattan Staff. Mental health was operationally defined by this research team as a measurable continuum ranging from good (low scores on the scale) to poor (high scores on the scale) (Langer, 1962, pp. 229-276).

Findings of the 22-Item Screening Score have been found to be strongly correlated with personal evaluations made by the psychiatrists on the Midtown Manhattan Staff (Langer, 1962). However, it was never intended that the 22-Item Screening Score be construed as a substitute for a psychiatrist's diagnosis of an individual patient since it was not constructed to detect organic brain damage, mental retardation, or sociopaths, nor the dimensions of anger, depression, anxiety, acting out, suspicion, hallucinating, delusion formation, memory loss, or concentration difficulty (Seiler, 1973, p. 252).

The Midtown researchers have reported that the 22-Items constituting the Mental Health Scale were selected from approximately 120 symptoms, which were principally derived from the Minnesota Multiphasic Personality

Inventory and the Neuropsychiatric Screening Adjunct. The original 120

symptoms were selected for inclusion in the Midtown questionnaire on several

bases. Many were considered to be typical of the complaints which a psychia-

trist hears in his practice. Other items were included because they seemed

to tap areas of disorders which were important to the Midtown researchers.

Finally, the largest group of items were included because they passed a

standard test of validity. The 22 items finally selected were chosen from

among the 120 because they were all shown to discriminate strongly between

two criterion groups: a "known well" group, and a "known ill" group of

Midtown residents. (See Langer, 1962, p. 270, for the method used in

selecting these two groups.) Langer reported that the 22 items all discrimi-

nated between the ill and well groups at the .01 probability level or better.

The 22-item scale consists of closed-ended questions which ask for

self-reported psychological, psychophysiological and physiological type

complaints. Examples of typical items (with pathognomic responses indicated

by an asterisk) are as follows:

ITEM	RESPONSE
I feel weak all over much of the time.	*1. Yes 2. No 3. Don't know 4. No answer
I have had periods of days, weeks or months when I couldn't take care of things because I couldn't "get going."	*1. Yes 2. No 3. Don't know 4. No answer

ITEM	RESPONSE
I have periods of such great restlessness that I cannot sit long in a chair (cannot sit still very long).	*1. Yes 2. No 3. Don't know 4. No answer

In establishing cut-off points to differentiate between normals, mildly impaired and severely impaired respondents on the basis of scores from the 22-Item Screening Score, the following procedure was followed by the Midtown Manhatten Staff. Scores from the 22-Item Screening Score were compared with classifications made by the Midtown study psychiatrists, and a cut-off point of four or more was determined to be the dividing line between "well" and "impaired." Of those respondents classified by the psychiatrists as "incapacitated" (serious symptoms with great impairment and total impairment), 84 percent had a score of four or over on the 22-Item Screening Score; whereas, of those classified as "well" only 1 percent had a score of four or over. Langer (1962) concluded that scores of four or over have a good probability of indicating present psychopathology (pp. 274-275).

Questions about the cut-off score used by Langer and also the construct validity of the 22-Item Scale as a measure of mental illness have been raised by various researchers, i.e., Manis, et al. (1963), Haese and Meile (1967), etc. Seiler (1973) perhaps summed it up best with this observation:

> Throughout the 22-Item Scale's history there are those who have defended its use, those who have criticized it, and others

who have fallen somewhere between (p. 253).

Several epidemiological scales and measures besides the 22-Item Scale have been utilized by researchers concerned with studies of mental illness, i.e., the instrument used in the Nationwide Study (Gurin, et al., 1960); the Health Opinion Survey (Macmillan, 1957) used in the Stirling County Study (Leighton, 1959; Hughes, et al., 1960; Leighton, et al., 1963); and the psychological distress items used in the U. S. National Health Survey (1960) (Seiler, 1973, p. 252).

The 22-Item Scale was chosen for inclusion in the original questionnaire because it is one of the most widely used scales in field studies of mental illness. Advantages of the scale lie in its value as a research instrument for screening large population groups for psychological stress that may be viewed as potential psychiatric cases, and/or in comparing population sub-groups directly with a view to deriving etiological clues. A second kind of advantage is its relative ease of administration and thirdly its economy when compared with the prohibitive cost of hiring social workers or psychiatrists to diagnostically evaluate each individual subject in a large-scale survey. Finally, the reliability and validity of the scale for measuring psychological stress is noteworthy, as previously mentioned (Manis, 1963, pp. 108-116).

The fact that recent research, Dohrenwend (1971) and Seiler and Summers (1972) have provided some evidence to support the contention that the Scale is not unidimensional but, in fact two scales; one that indicates

55

psychological stress, and the other physiological malaise (Seiler, 1973, p. 261) does not hinder its use for the purposes of this study which is to explore the association between family integration and the prevalence of psychological stress which may lead to psychiatric symptoms in heads of households. Since this study does not concern itself with diagnostic efforts to label psychological dysfunctions, these "shortcomings" of the scale as defined by Seiler (1973, p. 256) do not hamper its ability to provide a measure of psychological stress. Despite the somewhat overall critical evaluation of the scale made by Seiler, he still concluded that although the scale was not "an ideal measure," it does measure psychological stress and physical malaise (Seiler, 1973, p. 252).

For the purposes of this study, scores of one through three were coded "normal," four through six as "mildly impaired," and seven through the highest as "severely impaired." Respondent's scale scores were derived by dichotomizing replies into "pathognomic" and "non-pathognomic" categories and adding to get a total score of pathognomic answers.

Method of Data Analysis

The responses from the scales were coded and punched on tabulation cards for analysis using the Univac 1108 computer located in the University of Utah Computer Center. The Statistical Package for the Social Sciences (SPSS) was used in analyzing the data (Nie, Bent and Hull, 1970).

Both descriptive and inferential statistics were used including measures for correlation and multiple regression. Strength of relationship and significance were measured by Beta and Chi Square respectively. Beta (standardized regression coefficient) was generated in order to determine the effect of each independent variable: family integration, sex, job satisfaction, number of children, SES, stress, and alienation on psychiatric symptoms. The .05 level of significance was used.

CHAPTER IV

PRESENTATION AND ANALYSIS OF DATA

Psycho-Social and Demographical Variables

The preceeding chapters have described the problem of the study and how it fits within the context of interactionally based research. A review of research and theory in the area of family and mental health studies led to the adaptation of previously tested research assumptions to include further theory regarding the role of family based psychological stress in mental illness. With these theoretical assumptions as guides, hypotheses were formulated to test the adequacy of the proposed theoretical framework in helping to explain the association between family integration and mental illness. The remaining two chapters of this study were devoted to reporting, analyzing and discussing the findings of this study along with recommendations for future research.

The purpose of the study was to investigate the influence of high or low levels of family integration on the presence of psychiatric symptoms in heads of households. This was an attempt to find more empirical data to explain the interactional (psycho-social) or demographical components of psychological stress that may foster psychological maladjustment. The primary focus for the study was on the independent variable of family integration. High scores on Cavan's Scale for Rating Family Integration and Adaptability were seen as indicative of that kind of supportive familial atmosphere which would minimize psychological stress that may lead to mental illness. Conversely, low scores in family integration were viewed as indicative of a familial psycho-social interior more apt to produce that kind of psychological stress that may foster psychiatric symptoms in its members.

The dependent variable of psychiatric symptoms was measured by the 22-Item Screening Score of Psychiatric Symptoms Indicating Impairment. As a check on the validity of the 22-Item Screening Score as a measure of psychological stress, crosstabs were run on several variables. All of the variables that would normally be seen as symptoms of psychological stress, i.e., depression, anomie, alienation, powerlessness, normlessness, anxiety, hypochondriasis, stress scores and so forth, showed significant relationship (.05) to the 22-Item Screening Score. The reliability and validity of this scale was further described in Chapter III.

Independent Variables

A discussion of each of the independent variables of the study follows:

Family Integration

The interactional or psycho-social components of mental illness have long been recognized and increasingly stressed in social psychiatric mental health studies. The family system especially has come under scrutiny from researchers from various disciplines who have sought to understand the impact that socialization and family interaction has upon the mental health of family members (Lidz, 1957, 1958, 1963; Ackerman, 1958; Meissner, 1964; Handel, 1967; Henry, 1971; Satir, 1972; Skolnick, 1973). These studies collectively support the theoretical importance of the family's emotional and psychological atmosphere as a prime factor in the psychological adjustment of all the members within that particular family system. Lidz (1957, 1958, 1963) especially has researched the "intrafamilial environment" of schizophrenic patients in efforts to factor out what kinds of interaction are involved in pathogenic gamilies as opposed to families without psychotic members. Henry (1971) spent time as a participant observer within families with one psychotic member to support his contention that:

> . . . direct observation of families in their native habitat, going about their usual business, will furnish new insights into psychotic breakdown and other forms of emotional illness, and suggest new ideas for prevention and treatment (p. xv).

Schatzman (1973) wrote that people "learn strange patterns of experience and behavior early in life . . . as responses to maddening families" (p. xxi). These families were labeled by Schatzman as "models of madness". Howells (1971), in describing the phenomenon of psychic contagion remarked on the "ominous tendency of pathology to spread in both the horizontal (to interacting members of a specific family) and the vertical (intergenerationally)" (p. 396).

This study, by focusing on family integration as one of the independent variables, attempted to isolate the effect of this family factor on the mental health of heads of households. The operational measure used for this independent variable was Cavan's Scale for Rating Family Integration and Adaptability. (The details of this scale were described in Chapter III.)

Sex

A differential incidence of psychiatric impairment due to sex has been the research focus of many studies (Langer and Michael, 1963; Leighton, et al., 1963; Phillips, 1966; David, 1967; LeMasters, 1969; Laws, 1971; Gove, 1972). Research findings are not consistent, however, with some data supporting the contention that women are psychiatrically disturbed more frequently than men (Langer and Michael, 1963; Leighton, et al., 1963; Phillips, 1966; Laws, 1971; Gove, 1972) especially within the context of marriage. However, LeMasters' 1969 study claimed that men suffer more physical and/or psychological damage from marital strain than women. That contention was diametrically opposed to explanations to support the view that men suffer less psychiatric damage in troubled marriages and poorly integrated families given by David (1967) and Phillips and Segal (1960).

The above disparities of opinion both have logical and statistical support. David (1967) suggested that the husband is, generally speaking, apt to be less integrated into the family system than the wife (p. 217). This position of less intense involvement in family process may be an explanatory factor in the seemingly lower incidence of mental illness among male heads of households. Conversely, LeMasters (1969) postulated that women suffered less damage in chronically troubled families because they had more socially accepted channels for sublimating -- "substitute satisfactions" -- that are more in line with the basic values of the society (p. 437).

Another explanation for differences in self-reported psychiatric symptom levels due to sex was given by Phillips and Segal (1960) who suggested that women may report more symptoms than men since they are culturally conditioned to express feelings and share problems, whereas men might be more reticent to report symptoms due to their cultural scripting in the opposite direction. This is illustrative of one of the problems inherent in the self report method of data collection. It is impossible to tell whether such reports reflect real differences or only differences in peoples' willingness to report (Maccoby and Jacklin, 1974, p. iii).

Certainly, existing discrepancies in study findings reinforce the contention that more research is needed on this complex question of the relationship of sex as an independent variable on the development of psychiatric symptoms. This study was particularly interested in exploring that relationship taking into account family factors and whether poor interaction and integration within the family would have a differential impact on the mental health of men and women.

Number of Children

Folk wisdom has long advocated that having children is an iron-clad way to cement a failing marital union and keep a troubled family together. Empirical research, however, does not corroborate this homey advice (Campbell, 1975). To the contrary, the addition of children and the demands of a parental role often add loss of companionship and extra stress to the already existing problems of the marital relationship. This may lead to a further deterioration in the relationship and the increased possibility that the added psychological stress may foster the development of psychiatric symptoms in heads of households.

> Almost as soon as a couple has children, their happy bubble bursts. For both men and women, reports of happiness and satisfaction drop to average, not to rise again significantly until their children are grown and about to leave the nest (age 18) (Campbell, 1975, p. 39).

Whether there is an increasing or decreasing risk of added psychological stress as the number of children in a family grows larger, is another question this study addressed.

Job Satisfaction

In a 1970 article in the San Francisco Chronicle, psychiatrists Beisser and Glasser of University of California in Los Angeles reported research findings citing marital stress and job stress as the two primary precipitating factors in mental breakdown. This would support Meyers and Bean's 1968 study finding that persons who were poorly adjusted occupationally were also more apt to be psychiatrically impaired. Several studies have noted the relationship between job satisfaction and marital adjustment which by some family theorists is a construct that is interchangeable with family integration. It seems common sense to assume that people who were under occupational stress would suffer damage to the essential psychichal condition just as assuredly as they would under conditions of exposure to interactionally based familial stress. This independent variable then was seen as an important one to test in order to ascertain the relationship that it may have to the incidence of psychiatric symptoms in heads of households.

The Brayfield and Rothe Index of Job Satisfaction was used to measure this independent variable. The index contains 18 items scored by the Thurstone scoring system of five categories: (1) strongly agree, (2) agree, (3) undecided, (4) disagree, and (5) strongly disagree. A high total score on the index would represent high job satisfaction. The index has a Spearman-Brown reliability coefficient of .87. There is evidence supporting the high validity of the index since scores on the Brayfield and Roth Index of Job Satisfaction correlated .92 with scores on the Hoppock job satisfaction scale (Miller, 1964, p. 189).

Socioeconomic Status

Many studies seeking the etiological variables of mental illness cite social class as a prime factor (Hollingshead and Redlich, 1958; Srole, et al., 1962; Dohrenwend and Dohrenwend, 1969; Meyers and Roberts, 1959; and

Meyers and Bean, 1968). Most of these studies support the thesis that there is proportionately a greater amount of "severe" mental illness in the lower classes. A recent study, however, has applied more sophisticated statistical tests (Hogarty and Katz, 1971) and its findings suggest that the independent effect of social class explains only one percent of the variance in psychiatric symptoms. Data such as this that seemingly contradict previously corroborated research findings call for more research.

In this study a respondent's socioeconomic status was defined by rank position on the Hollingshead Index of Social Position. In describing the Two-Factor Index of Social Position, Hollingshead (1957) wrote:

> The Two-Factor Index of Social Position was developed to meet the need for an objective, easily applicable procedure to estimate the positions individuals occupy in the status structure of our society. Its development was dependent both upon detailed knowledge of the social structure, and procedures social scientists have used to delineate class position. It is premised upon three assumptions: (1) the existence of a status structure in the society; (2) positions in this structure are determined mainly by a few commonly accepted symbolic characteristics; and (3) the characteristics symbolic of status may be scaled and combined by the use of statistical procedures so that a researcher can quickly, reliably, and meaningfully stratify the population under study.

> Occupation and education are the two factors utilized to determine social position. Occupation is presumed to reflect the skill and power individuals possess as they perform the many maintenance functions in society. Education is believed to reflect not only knowledge, but also cultural tastes. The proper combination of these factors by the use of statistical techniques enable a researcher to determine within approximate limits the social position an individual occupies in the status structure of our society (p. 2).

The method used for calculating the Index of Social Position in this study followed the techniques presented by Hollingshead. During the interview, the respondents were asked to report the last grade of school completed with the possibilities ranging from one year of education to postgraduate work. They were also asked to indicate any other business, trade or other additional education. Occupation was determined by asking the subjects to name the type of work of the household head. In the majority of cases, this was the occupation of the husband. The use of the husband's occupation in this manner has been justified by Lenski (1954):

> . . . current literature, both theory and research indicates that the family is normally a status unit and that the social attributes of the family head are the chief determinants of status for all dependent relatives in the domicile (p. 407).

The validity of the Two-Factor Index of Social Position has been discussed by Hollingshead (1958), who has noted that:

> The assumption of a meaningful correspondence between an estimated class position of individuals and their social behavior has been validated by the use of factor analysis (pp. 398-407).

Alienation

A respondent's alienation was operationally defined by the total score on Dwight Dean's Alienation Scale (Dean, 1961, pp. 753-758). The Alienation Scale is made up of three sub-scales: powerlessness, normlessness and social isolation. Each of these sub-scales are considered symptomatic of psychological non-well-being. Therefore, as an independent variable, it would be anticipated that a high total score in alienation would explain some of the variance in the dependent variable of this study.

Dean has described the alienation scale and its three components as follows:

>Typical of the nine items in the final scale for <u>Powerlessness</u> were:
>"There is little or nothing I can do towards preventing a major 'shooting' war."
>"We are just so many cogs in the machinery of life."
>Reliability of this sub-scale, tested by the "split-half" technique, was .78 (N=384) when correlated by the Spearman-Brown prophecy formula.
>Typical of the six items in the <u>Normlessness</u> scale, constructed simultaneously by the same method, were:
>"The end often justifies the means."
>"I often wonder what the meaning of life really is."
>The reliability on this sub-scale, when corrected, was .73.
>Typical of the nine items of the <u>Social Isolation</u> sub-scale were:
>"Sometimes I feel all alone in the world."
>"One can always find friends if he shows himself friendly."
>The Social Isolation sub-scale had a "split half" reliability of .84 when corrected for attenuation.
>The three sub-scales were combined to make up the Alienation scale, which thus consisted of 24 items. The items from each of the sub-scales were rotated in order to minimize the possibility of halo effect. The total Alienation scale had a reliability of .78 when corrected (Dean, 1961, pp. 753-758).

Stress

The concept of stress has not been adequately or precisely defined in the behavioral sciences. In general, it seems to signify a state of affairs characterized by anxiety, discomfort, emotional tension, and difficulty in adjustment; it may be temporary and situational, or protracted and recurrent. In the present study, stress was operationally defined as the subject's report of the frequency with which he was bothered by "loneliness" and "nervousness". These were chosen as indicators of stress because they appear to be closely associated with self-concern, sensitivity to environmental threats, and difficulties in dealing with relatively routine life situations.

Nervousness, on the other hand, may reflect concern with performance, and the anticipation of possible failure in those areas of life where high aspirations have been set. Moreover, both loneliness and nervousness imply excessive self-concern and the latter may augment the former by trapping the person in a "vicious circle". A case in point would be the person who is so concerned about the adequacy of his performance that his nervousness intereferes with his ability to do well. Implicit in what has been said is the assumption that perception of a situation as nervous and lonely is itself stressful.

Accordingly, the measure used for this variable in this study was mechanic's stress scale which consisted of the following two questions:

> During the past year, how often were you bothered by:
> 1. Nervousness
>   Very often_____ Fairly often_____ Not very often_____
>   Never_____
> 2. Loneliness
>   Very often_____ Fairly often_____ Not very often_____
>   Never_____

Responses to these questions were combined to yield a total stress score. The population was then divided into the following groups:

> (1) High stress group: Persons who reported that they were both lonely and nervous, either very or fairly often.
>
> (2) Medium high stress group: Persons who reported either (a) that they were bothered very or fairly often by one,

and not very often by the other; or (b) that they were bothered very often by one but never by the other.

(3) Medium low stress group: (a) They were not bothered very often by loneliness or nervousness; or (b) that they were never bothered by one, and not very often by the other; or (c) that they were bothered fairly often by one but never by the other.

(4) Low stress group: Persons who reported that they were never bothered by either loneliness or nervousness.

In order to evaluate the validity of this index, the responses were compared with regard to such other responses as might be regarded as individual stress: worry, difficulty in college, general dissatisfaction, perception of the college environment as stressful, and being troubled by aches, indigestion and inability to sleep. Statistically significant relationships, at better than the .001 level, were found between the Mechanic stress scale and all of the above symptoms of stress. It can be said with some confidence, therefore, that the Mechanic stress scale does provide a valid measure of various levels of situational stress.

Testing the Hypotheses of the Study

The purpose of the remainder of this chapter will be to test the hypotheses of this study and to present and analyze the data collected. For convenience, the hypotheses are repeated below:

1. Persons living in families with lower scores in family integration will have significantly more psychological stress and psychiatric symptoms

than those persons who live in families with a higher level of family integration.

2. Controlling for marital status, persons living with a spouse and having lower scores in family integration will have significantly more psychiatric symptoms than persons who are divorced, widowed or married but separated.

3. Women with low scores in family integration will have significantly more psychological stress and psychiatric symptoms than will men with low scores in family integration.

4. Level of family integration will still be predictive of psychiatric symptoms when other social and demographical variables analyzed are held constant.

Hypothesis No. 1

The first hypothesis of this study stated that persons living in families with lower scores in family integration would have significantly more psychiatric symptoms than those persons who lived in families with a higher level of family integration. In order to test this hypothesis, the data from the 22-Item Score of Psychiatric Symptoms Indicating Impairment was cross tabulated with the data gathered by the Cavan Scale for Rating Family Integration and Adaptability. Findings related to this hypothesis are presented in Table 1.

Table 1

Psychiatric Symptoms by Family Integration
in Percentages

| Psychiatric Symptoms | Family Integration | | Totals |
	Low	High	
Normal	54.6 (83)	76.1 (166)	67.3 (249)
Mildly Impaired	28.3 (43)	17.0 (37)	21.6 (80)
Severly Impaired	17.1 (26)	6.9 (15)	11.1 (41)
Total Percent	100.0 (152)	100.0 (218)	100.0 (370)

X^2 (2df) = 19.68   P < .001
C = .31

As may be seen in Table 1, most people in the sample were "normal" (67 percent). This seems consoling since Charney (1972) asserted that "eighty to ninety percent of the population show up as starkly emotionally disordered" (p. 72). Table 2 illustrates the distribution of scores on the 22-Item Scale in Midtown Manhattan, New Hampshire and Utah. The concordance between scores shown on this table justify rejecting Charney's alarming assertion about the lack of quality of mental health as grossly exaggerated. Utah's percent of population scored as "severely impaired" is almost exactly the same as that found in the Midtown Manhattan Study (Phillips, 1966, p. 37).

Table 2

Distribution of Scores on the 22-Item Scale in Midtown
Manhattan, New Hampshire and Utah

Mental Health Score	Midtown Manhattan [a] (N=1660)	New Hampshire [a] (N=600)	Utah (N=370)
Percent with Scores of 4 or Over	31.20	27.50	21.60
Percent with Scores of 7 or Over	11.20	8.70	11.1

[a]Percentage Distribution of Scores in the Midtown Manhattan and New Hampshire Studies may be found in Derek L. Phillips, "The 'True Prevalence' of Mental Illness in a New England State," Community Mental Health Journal, 1966, 2, Table 1, p. 37.

As may be seen in Table 1, of the 370 respondents who completed both the family integration and the psychiatric symptoms scales, 55 percent of those with low family integration were in the normal range as compared to 76 percent who had higher scores in family integration. Forty-four percent of the heads of household who lived in poorly integrated families were in the impaired range as compared to 24 percent who had better integrated families. The most startling difference is in the "severely impaired" category. Here, persons living in families with low scores in family integration had over twice the chance (17 percent) of developing enough psychiatric symptoms to warrant their being classified as "severely impaired" as did those persons who lived in well integrated families (7 percent). Since the probability of receiving a computed X^2 of 19.98 is less than .001 and the correlation between family integration and psychiatric symptoms is -.21, it may be concluded that the number of symptoms a person has is inversely related to the level of family integration in the family in which he lives.

Without a longitudinal component in the study, it was impossible to determine whether people with more psychiatric symptoms had created families that were poorly integrated or conversely, whether the poor integration within the family had created psychological stress which fostered the development of psychiatric symptoms in family members. However, these study findings do provide initial support for the first hypotheses of the study.

Hypothesis No. 2

The second hypothesis of this study asserted that persons living with a spouse and having lower scores in family integration would have significantly more psychiatric symptoms than those persons who are divorced, widowed or married but separated. This assumption was based on the writer's belief that a change in a dysfunctional marital status would be reflected in an upsurge of psychological relief and well-being. Once a separation or divorce is achieved in a family that has been characterized by psychological stress and low family integration, it was anticipated that the respondent would be freed from a situation of excessive stress and would experience fewer psychiatric symptoms. This view is illustrated in Figure 1.

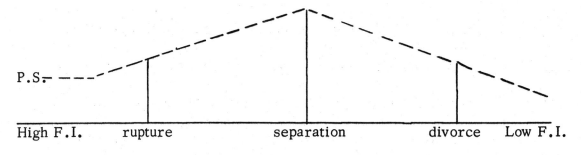

Figure 1

Suggested Relationship Between Family Integration
and Psychiatric Symptoms

As suggested in Figure 1, stress and psychiatric symptoms increase as families move toward disintegration. When interaction becomes so strained that relationships are ruptured, psychiatric symptoms take a sharp upward trend. At the point of separation or divorce, indicators of psychiatric disturbance decrease in response to the person's being removed from a situation of interactional and psychic stress. Study findings by Renne (1971) support this kind of reasoning since she found that unhappily married people were less healthy than either divorced or separated people of the same sex and age.

As can be seen in Table 3, the data of this study failed to support Hypothesis 2 and disagreed with earlier studies that asserted that united unhappy homes resulted in poorer adjustment scores (physically and/or psychologically) for parents as well as children than scores of persons from broken homes (LeMasters, 1969; Renne, 1971; Nye, 1959). The difference between the categories of "married living with spouse" and "divorced, widowed or separated", in terms of psychiatric impairment with low levels of family integration were not significant (17 percent as compared to 20 per-

cent).

Table 3

Psychiatric Symptoms by Family Integration and
Marital Status in Percentages

Psychiatric Symptoms	Married and Living with Spouse		Divorced, Widowed or Married but Separated		Totals
	Low F.I.	High F.I.	Low F.I.	High F.I.	
Normal	55.3 (73)	78.1 (146)	50.0 (10)	67.9 (19)	67.6 (248)
Mildly Impaired	28.0 (37)	16.0 (30)	30.0 (6)	21.4 (6)	21.5 (79)
Severely Impaired	16.7 (22)	5.9 (11)	20.0 (4)	10.7 (3)	10.9 (40)
Total Percent	100.0 (132)	100.0 (187)	100.0 (20)	100.0 (28)	100.0 (367)

Within categories, however, bigger differences are found. For

example, of those respondents, married and living with spouse, who had low

family integration, almost three times as many were categorized as "severely

impaired" as compared to those with a high level of family integration. In the

divorced, widowed, or separated category, there were more than two times

the number (20%) with low family integration who were severely impaired as

opposed to 11 percent who reported a high level of family integration. These findings support the relationship between family integration and psychiatric symptoms reported in Table 1, but also show that marital status may not be a good predictor of psychiatric symptoms.

In searching for an explanation for the apparent lack of affirmation between the data of this study and Hypothesis 2, it became apparent that the element of time could be an intervening variable. Without a test, re-test component in the study it was impossible to determine whether divorce leads to a decrease in family integration or makes it possible for a new integration within a closer family system. It may very well be that the inability to determine how long a respondent had been divorced, "washed out" the causative effects of divorce in terms of release from a situation of psychological stress and a decrease in psychiatric symptoms.

As can be seen in Figure 2, family integration decreases to a point of divorce then, plausibly, an individual could make a new life adjustment with a more closely integrated family system. Renne (1971) did find that persons who had remarried happily had fewer psychological and physical problems than those who remained in unhappy homes:

> Once they (the divorced) have gone through the period of dis-
> location associated with separation, divorcés are probably more
> likely to make new friends or maintain old ones than they were
> when they were handicapped by their unhappy marriages (p. 343).

It is also not unusual for divorced parents to have a closer relation-ship with children after the marital strife has been ended -- hence, some divorced persons might feel closer ties of family integration than those who are still married but emotionally isolated due to relationship stress.

It is apparent, therefore, that it would be of the utmost importance for one to know how long the respondent had been divorced since a measurement at point A in Figure 2 would reflect less re-integration in a family unit after divorce than would be possible over more time, represented in Figure 2 at point B. Assuming the inverse relationship between family integration and psychiatric symptoms suggested in Table 1, a similar graph illustrating the changing level of psychiatric symptoms after divorce is shown in Figure 3.

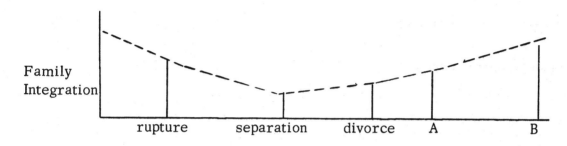

Figure 2

Illustration of Level of Family Integration After
Divorce

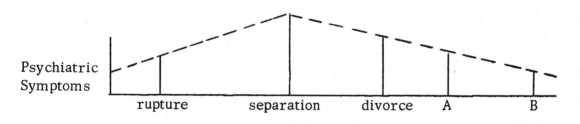

Figure 3

Illustration of Level of Psychiatric Symptoms
After Divorce

77

As illustrated in Figure 3, psychiatric symptoms would peak at the point of separation and then receed over time after divorce (represented by points A and B), when the individual begins to reintegrate into another family system. If the relationship between family integration and psychiatric symptoms suggested by Renne (1971) and illustrated in Figures 2 and 3 is correct, then it would be impossible to test Hypothesis 2 unless we could know at which point in time (A or B) that the divorced respondent was measured.

It must be concluded that Hypothesis 2 was not adequately tested in this study due to several limitations on the data: (1) as stated above, there was no way to ascertain length of time that the respondents had been separated or divorced, so time could be an intervening variable; (2) the number of cases in some categories were so small that it would be impossible to generalize findings with any degree of confidence; (3) since there was no test, re-test over time, it was impossible to determine whether being divorced had led to an increase or decrease in psychiatric symptoms; (4) there was no way to determine whether the severed relationship had been viewed by the respondents as a positive or a negative one, and hence, no way to determine whether the termination of that relationship was lamented or celebrated; (5) the collapsing of data to include divorced, widowed and married but separated in one category was not a wise choice since the circumstances around being widowed would be dissimilar in many respects from the other two methods of terminating relationships, and thus, different in its effects upon the respondents, (6) sex may be another intervening variable since recent study findings have shown that 25 percent of men report life as "difficult" after divorce as compared to 42 percent of women who find that increased family and work responsibilities after divorce (with only 4 percent able to hire extra household help) makes life after divorce "difficult" for them (Campbell, 1975, p. 43); and finally, (7) the age of the respondent, or "life stage" he or she is in at the time measured may be even more important than considerations of sex or marital status (Campbell, 1975, p. 43).

To understand how people feel about their lives, it is less important to know whether a person is a woman than to know whether she is a young, childless wife or a single career woman or married with grown children. We can't assume that all men view their lives as rich and fulfilling, either; we must know first whether the man is an aging bachelor or an empty-nest father (p. 45).

The assumptions underlying Hypothesis 2 warrant further research attention controlling for the factors mentioned above. Since the data of this study failed to accurately test Hypothesis 2, it can neither be accepted nor rejected.

Hypothesis No. 3

The third hypothesis of this study asserted that there would be a differential impact of low family integration for the two sexes. In LeMasters' (1969) study he wrote that he had the "distinct impression" that husbands are more likely to be severely damaged by chronic marital failure than are the wives (p. 437). However, the old saying that "the woman pays" was supported by the studies of Laws (1971) and Gove (1972).

Laws' (1971) data showed, "a case could be made that marriage is

not good for women" (p. 510) and Gove (1972) stated that the reason married

women had more mental illness than women who were widowed, divorced or

single could be attributed to the role of the married woman which was basically

"fragile" and frustrating due to its unstructured nature, often leaving women

with "expectations" that are unclear and diffuse (p. 34). Murstein and Glaudin

(1966) also saw women as having more at stake in the marriage than men

since, "For most women, marriage is a vocational role as well as a personal

relationship" (p. 43).

Data in Table 4 seem to support the contention of Hypothesis 3 that mar-

ried women, on the average, suffer more psychological damage in poorly

integrated families than do men. This is especially apparent in the severely

impaired category where 36 percent of women with low scores in family inte-

gration had scores on the 22-Item Scale sufficiently high to place them into

the "severely impaired" category as compared to only 16 percent of the men

with similar scores. These findings would provide initial support to the fourth

hypothesis of the study and call into question LeMasters' (1969) contention that

women suffer less psychological damage than men in a poorly integrated

family because they have developed more socially acceptable avenues for

sublimating. However, it would be premature on the basis of existing data

to make broad generalizations about this research question. One would need

to make other statistical comparisons and look at other combinations, i.e.,

married women vs. single women, before claiming to have conclusive data about the differential impact of marital status and family integration on the two sexes. The sparse response (N=3) from single respondents on the family integration scale made such further data analysis impossible in this study.

Table 4

Psychiatric Symptoms by Low Family Integration
and Sex in Percentages

| Psychiatric Symptoms | Low Family Integration | | Totals |
	Male	Female	
Normal	45.5	34.3	39.6
	(40)	(34)	(74)
Mildly Impaired	38.6	29.3	33.7
	(34)	(29)	(63)
Severely Impaired	15.9	36.4	26.7
	(14)	(36)	(50)
Total Percent	100.0	100.0	100.0
	(88)	(99)	(187)

X^2 (2df) = 9.95   P < .01

C = .22

Hypothesis No. 4

The fourth hypothesis of the study stated that level of family integration would be predictive of psychiatric symptoms when other social and demographical variables analyzed were held constant. To test this hypothesis a multiple regression analysis was employed.

Multiple regression analysis is an especially useful and practical statistical tool in behavioral research where there is one dependent variable but several independent variables. According to Kerlinger (1973):

> . . . Multiple regression analysis can be conceived as a refined and powerful method of "controlling" variance. It accomplishes this the same way analysis of variance does: by estimating the magnitudes of different sources of influence on Y, different sources of variance of Y, through analysis of the interrelations of all the variables. It tells how much of Y is presumably due to X_1, X_2 . . . X_k. It gives some idea of the relative amounts of influence of the X's. And it furnishes tests of the statistical significance of combined influences of X's on Y and of the separate influence of each X. In short, multiple regression analysis is an efficient and powerful hypothesis-testing and inference-making technique, since it helps the scientist study, with relative precision, complex interrelations between independent variables and a dependent variable, and thus helps him to "explain" the presumed phenomenon represented by the dependent variable (p. 631).

This study has seven independent variables (stress, family integration, job satisfaction, alienation, number of children, sex and SES) that were chosen as study variables because they were found to be significantly related to psychiatric symptoms or else to have such documented support in the research literature or theories of mental health as to warrant their further study. Given these seven independent variables and the research problem of Hypothesis 4, which was to determine which of the seven variables accounted for the most variance in the dependent variable of psychiatric symptoms, multiple regression analysis was indicated. The regression equation is used to provide an optimum prediction of the dependent variable (Nie, et al., 1970).

In Table 5, the relative amount of influence of each of the predictor variables on psychiatric symptoms can be seen. Analysis at the simple correlation level provides only a limited amount of information with regard to the importance of each independent variable as a predictor of psychiatric symptoms. Examining the simple correlation shows that stress with a correlation of -.58 has by far the highest correlation with psychiatric symptoms. This level of analysis, however, does not permit an understanding of the overall relationship between each of the independent variables and the dependent variable being measured, or the extent to which the development of psychiatric symptoms can be attributed to each of the seven would-be predictors. For this information one needs to proceed to analyze the data using multiple regression techniques. When each of the independent variables is considered relative to its overall contribution to the total regression, the directionality of their relationship is similar -- but stronger -- than that presented at the simple level of correlation.

As can be seen, stress, with a Beta weight of -.514 accounts for over a third of the total variance (34%) when the other independent variables are not in the equation. This finding was anticipated since stress is commonly viewed as being indicative of psychological disturbance. Stress by itself accounts for .336 of the variance, and is thus by far the best predictor of psychiatric symptoms. The addition of job satisfaction to the equation increases the R^2 to .387. Family integration is the third most important variable and when it is added the R^2 is increased to .403. Alienation's contribution to the equation is small, making the cumulative total .412. The other three variables, number of children, sex, and SES, do not add significantly to the total variance explained (41.4%). The residual or unexplained variance in psychiatric symptoms is 58.6 percent.

Table 5

Simple Correlation Coefficients and Betas for Each
Independent Variable and Psychiatric Symptoms

Psychiatric Symptoms	r	Beta
Stress	-.58	-.514**
Job Satisfaction	-.28	-.192**
Family Integration	-.21	-.104**
Alienation	.32	.107*
Number of Children	-.003	.040
Sex	.20	.023
SES	.06	.012

** P < .01

* P < .05

Surprisingly, job satisfaction has the second largest Beta (-.192). This variable has been isolated before as a predictor of psychiatric symptoms (Meyers and Bean, 1968; Beisser and Glasser, 1970) and therefore this study replicates these earlier findings. The results of this analysis of data would indicate the possibility that the Brayfield and Rothe Index of Job Satisfaction could be used to advantage by industrial counselors and others, not only to obtain a measure of job adjustment, but also as a way to ascertain the psychological well-being of workers.

Family integration, with a Beta of -.104 makes a significant contribution to the variance. In view of all the literature on the subject, one might anticipate a stronger relationship between family integration and psychiatric symptoms than is supported by the data of this study. Consequently, one could question the construct validity of the Cavan Scale in testing the qualitative aspects of family integration. For instance, a score on the amount of family activities shared tells us quantitatively how much or how often family members interact -- but not how that interaction affects the family member psychologically -- i.e., in a positive or negative direction.

Perhaps newer criteria need to be developed to more accurately measure the psycho-social interior of the family, such as: (1) internal role consistency among family members (relative absence of double-bind situations or mixed messages); (2) consistency of family roles and norms and actual performance (levels of trust and security); (3) compatibility of family roles and norms with community norms ("fit" in the world); (4) ability of the family to meet the psychological needs of family members (to be accepting and to individualize); and (5) the ability of the family group to respond to change (flexibility vs. rigidity) (Glasser and Glasser, 1970, p. 291). The use of such scale items in future research would perhaps provide a more qualitative assessment that could possibly get closer to a more effective measure of those processes within family life that promote or destroy mental health, and thus provide a more accurate picture of the importance of family factors in the development of psychiatric symptoms.

However, it may also be the case that the Cavan Scale is providing an accurate measurement of family integration and that the importance of the family in determining the mental health of its members has been exaggerated -- as was the case with SES. It may be that persons with unsupportive or pathological family factors learn to turn to others outside the family unit for psychological support and validation, and thus tend to escape or mitigate much of the supposedly negative influence of poor family integration on their psycho-social development.

Despite the small percentage of variance in psychiatric symptoms explained by the use of Cavan's Scale for Rating Family Integration and Adaptability, the relationship between family integration and psychiatric symptoms remained significant even when the effects of the other independent variables were held constant. Thus, Hypothesis 4 of this study could be accepted.

Earlier questions about whether the size of the family would have an effect on the psychological well-being of parents cannot be answered by the data in Table 5. By including Table 6 the results of the study with regard to this question can be seen. With a Beta of only .040, it is apparent that number of children is not a good predictor of psychiatric symptoms. Also, as shown in Table 6, there is little difference between "normals" (38%), "mildly impaired" (29%), and "severely impaired" (32%) when there is one child. With the addition of children (2+) there is still little evidence to indicate that having more children adds significantly to the probability of parents' becoming severely disturbed psychologically. At best, one could say that there is a slight tendency to peak at a position of being "mildly impaired" when more than one child is a part of the family unit.

Table 6

Psychiatric Symptoms by Low Family Integration
Number of Children in Percentages

| Psychiatric Symptoms | Low Family Integration | | Totals |
	One Child	2+	
Normal	38.2 (13)	29.2 (21)	32.1 (34)
Mildly Impaired	29.4 (10)	45.8 (33)	40.6 (43)
Severely Impaired	32.4 (11)	25.0 (18)	27.4 (29)
Total Percent	100.0 (34)	100.0 (72)	100.0 (106)

P = N.S.

Future research would do well to add to the study design on this question, ways to test the relationship between number of children and psychiatric symptoms in parents while considering the age of the children. It would be interesting to see if, in addition to differential impact with different numbers of children, there is also differential stress on parents due to the ages of their children, i.e., of teenagers (13-19), for instance, as compared to toddlers (1-5), or grade-schoolers (6-12), or even of the combined effect of having children in various age groups in one family at the same time. Such an analysis would provide a more definitive answer to the effects that children can have upon the mental health of heads of households. Also, there is recent research evidence to suggest that the age or "life stage" of the parent has a high correlation with the amount of child-related stress experienced, with married couples with small children reporting the greatest amount of stress and parents of older children among the happiest groups in the study (Campbell, 1975, pp. 34-39). According to this study by Campbell:

> Raising a family seems to be one of those tasks like losing weight or waxing the car, that is less fun to be doing than to have done (p. 38).

Neither sex or SES accounted for a significant amount of variance in psychiatric symptoms. These findings call into question long held views about females' being the more psychologically maladjusted sex, and the equally tenaciously held opinion that socio-economic status is, in and of itself, an important predictor of a differential psychiatric adjustment. It would be an interesting study question for future researchers to test whether the women's liberation movement has had an impact on bringing the sexes into a more equal participation in life, and thus led to an improvement in the over-all mental health of women. The study findings related to SES and psychiatric impairment seem to support Hogarty and Katz (1971) in their contention that the independent effect of social class explained only one percent of the variance in psychiatric symptoms.

Conclusions and Implications

The question as to what part family factors play in determining why some people develop psychiatric symptoms while others do not, is not answered in the descriptions and analysis of this study. The main interest has been to begin to empirically determine the influence, or lack of it, of family integration on the essential psychichal condition or mental health of heads of households. Although it cannot be claimed that this study proves that a person with a low score in family integration will be more likely to develop psychiatric symptoms, it can be claimed that the study does show an association between family integration and mental health. Through multiple regression, seven independent variables have been defined that account for about 41 percent of the variance in psychiatric symptoms.

The relationship between job satisfaction and psychiatric symptoms is such that it behooves business and industrial personnel to consider the practicality of making counseling more readily available to employees. The non-availability of help for those experiencing occupational stress was documented by Beisser and Glasser (1970) when they observed:

> The individual struggling with problems surrounding work apparently is reluctant to discuss them for fear of losing his job, or because such help is not available.

The findings of this study would support the assumption that a society's making counseling services available for familial and work related problems would be in the best interest of the mental health of its members.

CHAPTER V

SUMMARY, RESULTS AND RECOMMENDATIONS

Summary of Procedures

The present study was undertaken to explore the association between family integration and the prevalence of psychological stress that may lead to psychiatric symptoms in heads of household. The practical significance of this topic was emphasized by the findings of previous research which presented discontinuities to be clarified and gaps to be filled with regard to the place of the family in the etiology of mental illness. Also, the "Divorce Explosion" has reached such epidemic proportions that new insights into the effects of family disintegration upon mental health are needed. If the components of family life that promote good mental health can be more closely delineated, then marriage and family therapists will have more effective "tools" with which to help troubled families.

The position taken in this study was that having a low score in family integration would be indicative of family interaction conducive to the presence of psychological stress which may foster psychiatric symptoms. In this regard, theory and research on family socialization and interaction support the assumption that a disturbance in the essential psychichal condition through unsupportive family associations could produce feelings of non-validation and anxiety which could cause differential amounts of discomfort and psychological stress in family members. Lidz (1963) asserted this connection between family integration and the faulty mental development of its members when he wrote:

> It is my thesis that a large proportion of the failures of adequate ego integration arises in persons who have grown up in families which lacked proper integration because the parents' ways of interacting led to a faulty family organization deficient in these essentials (p. 54).

To test the assumptions of this study, seeking to scientifically understand the relationship between family integration and mental health, hypotheses were formulated. Basically, these hypotheses stated that the level of family integration had an inverse relationship with the prevalence of psychiatric symptoms and that marital status and sex were factors that needed to be taken into account when viewing the impact of family associations upon an individual member's mental health.

Data to empirically test the hypotheses were obtained from structured interviews with heads of households in Salt Lake City, Utah. Respondents were chosen by means of a two-stage systematic random sampling technique. Complete information was obtained on 370 of the total number of 578 respondents since 206 failed to complete the family integration scale. The two respondents who were single and who did complete the scale were not included in the analysis of data. In addition to information on the independent variable of family integration and the dependent variable of psychiatric symptoms, demographical data and information on a number of control variables was also gathered in the course of each interview.

Results

The tests of hypotheses and analysis of data led to the following findings of the study:

1. A low level of family integration has an inverse relationship to psychiatric symptomatology in heads of households.

2. Level of family integration is more predictive of psychiatric symptoms than is marital status.

3. Women develop more psychiatric symptoms in a poorly integrated family than do men.

4. Job satisfaction may be one of the best social or demographical predictors of psychiatric symptoms when variables clearly related to psychological stress are deleted.

Recommendations

The following observations and recommendations were generated by the review of literature as well as the study just completed. A vast amount of research recommendations related to family studies and mental health found in the literature still remain to be implemented. It seemed relevant to re-introduce and organize into one place past suggestions for future research along with observations growing out of the present study.

Gaps and Overlaps

Of all social phenomena, the human family ranks near
the top in the frequency and in the variety of perspectives with
which it has been studied (Turner, 1970, p. 3).

Tharpe (1965) stated that despite seventy years of marriage research

that there was available "but a small ground of knowledge" (p. 531). The

findings of this study have further exposed and explored some of the dis-

continuities in knowledge within the field of marriage and family research,

and has made some additions to existing theory. It remains the task of

future studies to design researchable hypotheses which will lead to the pro-

gressive elimination of yet remaining gaps and overlaps. Evidence indicates

that the conceptual framework of the interaction approach will be one of the

most fruitful to pursue:

The interactional approach has probably done more than
any other framework to remove family study from the realm of
speculation to the field of scientific study and analysis (Nye and
Berardo, 1966, p. 121).

Still, the research of the sixties, coming out of an interactional

framework but primarily concerned with marital adjustment, received its

share of criticism. The criticisms were grouped by Skolnick (1973) into

four general areas of concern. Paraphrased, these are: (1) the research

relied too heavily on self-reports; (2) one could argue with the assumption

that happiness is the criteria for good relationships; (3) there is a problem

in defining happiness as an absence of conflict and quarreling since an empty

shell marriage lacking in any communication (positive or negative) may not

94

be happy; and (4) "sick" or "neurotic interaction" type marriages may rate high on the marital adjustment scale if the two spouses seem to be satisfied with each other (pp. 208-215). Clearly, these criticisms need to be taken into consideration by future researchers in the family area.

Conceptual Difficulties

One of the primary tasks to be accomplished by future research into family life is to delimit the area of study. The complexity of this subject demands refinement of focus. Research about family dynamics must be separated from research primarily dealing with the marital pair. This delimitation becomes increasingly necessary as birth rates drop and more couples elect to remain childless.

Necessary also is a refining of concepts used in family research to take into consideration new findings. For example, it seems senseless to use terms like "stable," "unified," "cohesive," or "solidarity" as descriptions equated with healthy family life. Too many studies have shown that merely being together is not always indicative of positive family functioning. Where terms have been defined more specifically in the past to try to more clearly get at issues of family attitudes and functioning that may indicate a positive togetherness, i.e., Cavan's Scale for Rating Family Integration and Adaptability, care must be taken to avoid a criteria gap that can occur with changes in macro cultural conditions. For instance, it seems apparent that the character or essence of family integration may change as the family

95

responds to a changing culture with ever-changing values and attitudes. In the depression years of 1938, Angell's study reflected the larger society when he cited economic interdependence as one of three prime factors in family integration. Hill deleted that aspect of family integration completely from the scale when he studied the less economically interdependent family of 1949.

Another evolution in definition has occurred in the affectional area. In 1938 Cavan and Ranck saw one major element of family unity as:

> . . . the capacity of the family to satisfy within the family circle the personal interests of its members (pp. 2-5).

In the more liberal and mobile society of 1972, Nena and George O'Neill wrote of the necessity of allowing the freedom for family members to expand the circle of significant others to include those non-family members who might meet needs of different levels than family members are able to do (O'Neill and O'Neill, 1972). This represents a dramatically different view than the 1938 idea that a family's unity might depend on its ability to meet its members' needs within the closed system of the family circle. These changes in family orientations seem to point out the need for redefining and re-conceptualizing the criteria of family integration in ways that are not only clear and distinct but also dynamic enough in nature to remain relevant to ever-changing families.

A whole new typology is also needed for defining the family as a psychological unit and for labeling various kinds of marital interaction.

These needs are mentioned extensively in the literature. For example, in

the area of interpersonal relationships Schatzman (1973) wrote:

> Psychiatrists' nosology classifies individials psychiatrists
> see as disturbed but lacks categories for labeling the inter-
> personal situation that may be disturbing them. We need
> suitable idioms, schemas, and models with which to think
> about the effects on persons of social contexts -- families,
> schools, churches, factories, and clubs -- and about social
> relations between micro-social and small groups and their
> macro-social contexts -- society as a whole (p. 131).

The search for new conceptual ways to describe marital and familial

interactions has already begun, as evidenced by the Hicks and Platt (1970)

article:

> We need a comprehensive typology of marriages which
> permits predicting differentially for happy-stable, unhappy-
> stable, and unhappy-unstable marriages (p. 563).

The task remains for future researchers to conceptualize and

operationalize a more meaningful typology for family studies that will also

take into consideration the complexity of family life and the effects that the

adjustment of the marital pair has upon the mental health of all of the

family's members. Some research findings question the "healthiness"

of stereotyped role performance on the emotional well-being of both men

and women -- seeing this kind of molded behavior as negating the personhood

of each. Also, there are contradictory views reflected in the literature as

to whether family disintegration is an indicator of psychological disorder

within the family and/or the marital pair or whether psychological symptoms

are the result of family member's choosing to remain within the malfunctioning family system (LeMasters, 1969; Renne, 1971). Renne went so far as to suggest that:

> . . . failure to terminate an unhappy marriage may itself be an indicator of low ego strength. The relatively high (less neurotic) scores of divorced women and most divorced men may mean that people with 'stronger' or more resilient egos were more willing than others to break up their marriages (p. 342).

More research in this area is indicated to help resolve the questions of whether family disintegration and disharmony lead to personal disintegration and marital problems -- perhaps creating certain circumstances wherein divorce would be "therapeutic" (Gold, 1959) -- or whether lack of family integration and/or divorce in and of itself can be a cause of personal disorganization (Waller, 1930; 1951) and also to test the assertion that unhappily married people were on the whole more likely than the separated and divorced to display low ego strength (Renne, 1971, p. 342).

It has often been assumed in past studies that if a marriage was "adjusted" or "stable" that the family would be "healthy". These assumptions are being repeatedly challenged by many researchers and the problem has been succinctly described by Lidz (1963):

> In marriages which we have termed "skewed," the partners are reasonably well satisfied but the parental roles are unbalanced and deviant . . . Problems come when the addition of children sets limits upon the couple's ways of relating -- especially if they are to foster the proper development of their children (pp. 40-50).

Thus, marital partners who are "well satisfied" with each other, may still head a family that is dysfunctional for some of its members. With such complex factors involved, it is conceivable that one could begin to delimit differential effects of the same familial environment on the various members therein. For instance, a specific familial adjustment may provide a psycho-social interior in the family which: (1) functions effectively for the integration of the individual and of the group; (2) is effective for the individual but not for the group; (3) is effective or constructive for the family group but not for the individual member; (4) provides an environment that is damaging to both the individual and the family group.

LeMasters (1969), in an article entitled "Holy Deadlock: A Study of Unsuccessful Marriages," pointed out that his research indicated that couples with a long history of marital conflict (ten years minimum) were not able to ever "solve" their marital problems, and that these couples did not escape the destructive impact of marital failure by avoiding separation or divorce. In this study 78 percent of the respondents suffered "personal disorganization" over time, as manifested by alcoholism, psychosomatic illness, neurotic-psychotic behavior, occupational disorganization, extramarital affairs or disenchantment. It was suggested that the 25 percent who showed none of these symptoms of chronic marital failure had escaped such disorganization by employing at least three different coping mechanisms: (1) a higher capacity to tolerate frustration; (2) a displacement of hostility outside the primary family; or (3) because the couple learned how to avoid interaction by developing "separate worlds".

How to systematically make the conceptual differentiations that need to be made in order to conduct more meaningful studies where such complex issues are involved and where so many varying kinds of personalities and marital combinations are possible, is a real research challenge. Lidz (1963) has suggested that perhaps part of the problem in researching family factors affecting mental health is a need to first define what families must do to meet the affectional and developmental needs of its members:

> A clearer understanding gained through scientific scrutiny of the functions of the family and what is requisite to fulfill the needs of spouses and promote the harmonious development of offspring can help preserve the essentials while the family continues to change in a changing society (p. 38).

In seeking new typologies and psychological classifications for families it is clear once again that static descriptions are not adequate and that there will have to emerge "some conception of dynamic interplay among members" (Sussman, 1959, p. 523).

Cultural Considerations

Next to problems of conceptualization and closely related to the challenge for future research to take into account the impact of the larger culture upon the family and to try to determine ways to assess that impact. Even as far back as 1945 Burgess and Locke made a plea for such considerations in research design:

> Cultural conditions are related in integrating persons into the family structure. This has become an imperative problem for further study, a problem requiring the research techniques of psychiatrists and sociologists (p. 357).

In 1960 Parad and Caplan stressed the complicated "field of forces" represented in the family unit and asserted that it therefore required a three-dimensional perspective when studied, including: (1) the intra-personal; (2) the inter-personal; and (3) the supra-personal (p. 3).

Pinard (1966) also stressed the importance of recognizing the increasing effects of "common causes located outside the micro-world of the family system" (p. 568) upon family breakdown. Cavan and Ranck (1971) are other researchers who agreed with Burgess and Locke's contention that research was needed into "how psychological motivations and cultural conditions cooperate in integrating persons into the family structure" (p. x).

Methodological Recommendations

Time and again the literature reflects a need to move from self report as a method of gathering data to non-reactive measures. The problems with self report run the gamut from "no response" to responses that are grossly distorted or disparate. It is not uncommon to find that various family members have very different views of the family process and their part in it. Also, one must be aware that defense mechanisms like denial and projection can operate to invalidate observations of family members. All in all, one must doubt the validity of the exclusive use of self report as a way of gathering information about family interaction. The introduction of personal interview, as was the case in this study, is a step forward, but future researchers would do well to go even further to assure an objective viewing and analysis of the total family's interaction by family specialists. Such recommendations and observations were made as long ago as 1959:

Studying the whole family for its influence on an individual member's behavior and development, and for its own unique behavior as a unit is the most innovative suggestion made in the family field during the past decade (Sussman, 1959, p. 515).

Yet, as late as 1966, Nye and Berado stated:

There is a scarcity of studies which view all of the family members, i.e., husband-wife, or parent-child -- for a framework which sees the family as a unity of interacting personalities this appears to be an obvious gap (p. 121).

Longitudinal studies have also been suggested in the literature (Myers and Bean, 1968; Lipetz, 1970) but as yet, there are few to be found. Perhaps there is no answer to the riddle of which comes first -- the sick person who makes a sick family or the sick family that produces sick people. But, if an answer is to be found, it will perhaps require a research design in which newly married couples are tested then re-tested repeatedly over a twenty year span (Renne, 1971, p. 347).

A fourth recommendation for methodological consideration in future research would be to design studies to test some of the developing conceptual frameworks of family observers. For instance: (1) Henry's (1971) idea that certain "invariants" can be isolated and their presence or absence in families seen as indicators of health or pathology; (2) the suggestion that happy marriages and families are of two basic types -- an intrinsic or companionate marriage where the couples are more likely to concentrate on relationship sources of happiness, or a utilitarian or instrumental marriage where those reporting less happiness tend to concentrate on the situational aspects (home, children, social life) as sources of happiness (Hicks and Platt, 1970, pp.

560-563); (3) the notion of "static families" versus "transformative families" (Hess and Handel, 1956, p. 101); (4) the part family rituals may play in promoting a healthy family stability (Henry, 1971, p. 24; Bell and Vogel, 1960, p. 434); (5) types of communication within families and the importance of and differential impact of various forms of communicating on the health of family members (Schatzman, 1973, p. 92); and finally (6) some testing of Satir's (1972) theory around what distinguishes a "nurturing family" from a "troubled family":

> No matter what kind of problem first led a family into my office -- whether a nagging wife or an unfaithful husband, a delinquent son or a schizophrenic daughter -- I soon found that the prescription was the same. To relieve their family pain, some way had to be found to change those four key factors (self-worth, communication, rules, and link to society). In all of these troubled families I noticed that -- self worth was low; communication was indirect, vague, and not really honest; rules were rigid, inhuman, nonnegotiable, and everlasting; and the linking to society was fearful, placating, and blaming.

> Fortunately, I have also had the joy of knowing some un-troubled and nurturing families -- especially in my more recent workshops to help families develop more fully their potential as human beings. In these vital and nurturing families, I con-sistently see a different pattern -- self worth is high; communi-cation is direct, clear, specific, and honest; rules are flexible, human, appropriate, and subject to change; and the linking to society is open and hopeful (pp. 3-4).

These research recommendations do not purport to be comprehensive but only suggestive of several areas deserving consideration in future research designs; (1) away from self report; (2) studying the family as a dynamic interacting unit of diverse personalities; (3) longitudinal designs; and (4) the necessity for testing some of the existing conceptual frameworks. "We seemingly 'know' some things that promote mental health or illness within the interaction of the family unit, yet these pieces of "knowledge" need to be empirically tested, then validated, rejected or modified.

Prevention

The contention that prevention is easier, more economical and more effective than cure (Burgess and Locke, 1945, p. 426), would find few opponents. Yet little in the way of concrete steps have been taken to integrate existing knowledge and theory of family relationships to mental health into education, i.e., courtship and marriage classes, high school health classes, or premarital counseling programs. Surely future research should design studies to measure the effectiveness of various preventative methods with an eye toward making them more viable programs.

An innovative kind of prevention was suggested by Farson (1969) when he wrote of "inventing family futures" and creating "families by design" through utilizing existing social technologies (pp. 63-64 and 76). Also interested in raising the quality of family life is Satir (1964) who wrote of "family engineering". Certainly, this whole creative approach to preventing problems in family relationships by planning ahead deserves some research attention. Lidz (1963) and deRam (1965) have warned that:

> Scientific thinking demands a willingness to follow observation and reasoning wherever they may lead, unfettered by traditional beliefs (p. 26).

and:

Perhaps research may lead to adjustments in family
life beyond traditional life styles (p. 141).

A time might come when prevention would mean more than early

treatment, and more than putting a stop to conditions that foster psychiatric

disorder. It could come to mean developing certain kinds of environmental

conditions which have been demonstrated as favorable to mental health

within the family.

Summary

There is probably no greater cause of human unhappiness than dis-

torted and distorting family life. The importance of this first and most

consistent socializing agent upon mental health is only just beginning to be

explored in any real scientific kind of way. The social problems resulting

from broken homes and unbroken pathological homes illustrate the importance

of studies into the complex and dynamic nature of family integration and

pathogenesis.

This study has added a contribution to the growing body of theory in

the area of marriage and the family and mental health, but it also serves

to point out how much more data is needed in order to understand the part

that family interaction plays in the etiology and development of mental

illness.

Further research into these difficult issues can best be accomplished

by an interdisciplinary approach. Younghusband (1967) made a plea for a "rapprochment between social science and the disciplines such as casework and psychiatry," and argued for a "unified theory of human behavior" (p. 156). Cavan and Ranck (1971) also saw this as the way to go:

> Only the establishment of institutes of family research, bringing into one organization the different indispensable specialties, will provide the basic body of knowledge adequate for developing practical programs of assisting families to adjust to crises and to maintain their integrity under the changing conditions of modern life (p. x).

The challenge of understanding family life _will_ require the best of all existing family theories -- regardless of their source -- and increasingly more stringent research controls. Family theorists need to avoid both extremes of research -- the sweeping generalizations that have no detailed observation or testing to support them, or conversely -- the operationalizing and testing of trivia. The practical knowledge already accumulated by sociologists and family therapists needs to be implemented on behalf of families in pain. To defer implementation awaiting empirical verifications would place therapists in the "perduring problem of choice" described by Henry (1971):

> . . . between folded hands (wait until all the facts are in) and action based on knowledge conditioned by probable error (p. xxi).

As this project ends -- with some new answers, but so many unanswered questions left to be unraveled -- the observation of Leighton (1959) seems best to describe where theories related to interactional components of mental health are today:

. . . so many dangling questions are left. But then, life dangles; only conundrums have answers. Life flows in its arcs and streamers of multicolors, but it is not pulled together for us, it is not explained, and neither misery nor happiness are guaranteed. Lines are fixed only in death, madness, and fiction (p. 392).

APPENDICES

APPENDIX A

CAVAN'S SCALE FOR RATING FAMILY INTEGRATION AND ADAPTABILITY

The following questions apply to your family:

_____ 1. Indicate the amount of affection shared between your spouse and yourself. (1) Very hostile and tense relationship, (2) minor disagreements and aloofness, (3) "average", congenial and loyal, (4) in love more than average, (5) extremely affectionate.

_____ 2. What kind of relationship exists between your spouse and your children? (1) Much friction or great detachment, (2) some friction, favoritism or detachment, (3) "average", good relationship to all, (4) closer than average, (5) extremely close relations to all children.

_____ 3. What kind of relationship exists between yourself and the children? (1) Much friction or great detachment, (2) some friction, favoritism or detachment, (3) "average", good relationship to all, (4) closer than average, (5) extremely close relations to all children.

_____ 4. What kind of relationship exists between your children? (1) Great friction, (2) friction minor, but continuous, (3) "average", passing friction only, seldom, (4) closer than average, (5) all very cooperative and closely bound.

_____ 5. To what extent does your family engage in joint activities or discussions? (1) Almost none, most activities individual, (2) few family activities, many individual activities, (3) about equal number of family and individual activities, (4) many family activities, few individual activities, (5) most family activities, very few individual activities.

_____ 6. How much cooperation exists among your family members? (1) Refuse to cooperate or sacrifice, (2) reluctant to sacrifice or cooperate, (3) moderate sacrifices, but also maintain own interests, (4) willing to sacrifice, good cooperation, (5) extreme sacrifices for family, great amount of cooperation.

_____ 7. How would your family react to a problem which might create family tension? (1) Major strain on family, (2) minor but lasting tension, (3) "average", some pairing off, no lasting tension, (4) passing rivalries only, (5) no rivalries or antagonisms.

_____ 8. How does your family as a whole react to its economic situation? Does your family experience: (1) feeling tension, (2) some dissatisfaction, (3) no ill effect, (4) more than average unity, (5) extreme feeling of economic unity.

_____ 9. Indicate your present feeling toward your family. (1) Dislike style of family life, (2) accept family, but would like to make some changes, (3) "average", think family is all right, (4) good family pride, would resent criticism, (5) extreme pride in family style of living, in ancestors, etc.

_____ 10. How do you rate the happiness of your family? (1) Very unhappy, (2) unhappy, (3) average, (4) above average happiness, (5) very happy.

APPENDIX B

A TWENTY-TWO ITEM SCREENING SCORE OF
PSYCHIATRIC SYMPTOMS INDICATING
IMPAIRMENT [a]

Item	Response
1. I feel weak all over much of the time	*1. Yes[b] 2. No 3. DK[c] 4. NA[d]
2. I have had periods of days, weeks, or months when I couldn't take care of things because I couldn't "get going."	*1. Yes 2. No 3. DK 4. NA
3. In general, would you say that most of the time you are in high (very good) spirits, good spirits, low spirits, or very low spirits?	1. High 2. Good *3. Low *4. Very Low 5. DK 6. NA
4. Every so often I suddenly feel hot all over.	*1. Yes 2. No 3. DK 4. NA

[a]The scale items are quoted from Thomas S. Langer, "A Twenty-Two Item Screening Score of Psychiatric Symptoms Indicating Impairment," Journal of Health and Human Behavior, 3 (Winter, 1962), pp. 269-276.

[b]An asterisk indicates the scored or pathognomonic response.

[c]DK indicates Don't Know.

[d]NA indicates No Answer.

Item	Response
5. Have you ever been bothered by your heart beating hard? Would you say: often, sometimes, or never?	*1. Yes 2. No 3. DK 4. NA
6. Would you say your appetite is poor, fair, good or too good?	*1. Poor 2. Fair 3. Good 4. Too Good 5. DK 6. NA
7. I have periods of such great restlessness that I cannot sit long in a chair (cannot sit still very long).	*1. Yes 2. No 3. DK 4. NA
8. Are you the worrying type (a worrier)?	*1. Yes 2. No 3. DK 4. NA
9. Have you ever been bothered by shortness of breath when you were not exercising or working hard? Would you say: often, sometimes, or never?	*1. Often 2. Sometimes 3. Never 4. DK 5. NA
10. Are you ever bothered by nervousness (irritable, fidgety, tense)? Would you say: often, sometimes, or never?	*1. Often 2. Sometimes 3. Never 4. DK 5. NA
11. Have you ever had any fainting spells (lost consciousness)? Would you say: never, a few times, or more than a few times?	1. Never 2. A few times *3. More than a few times 4. DK 5. NA

Item	Response
12. Do you ever have any trouble in getting to sleep or staying asleep? Would you say: often, sometimes, or never?	*1. Often 2. Sometimes 3. Never 4. DK 5. NA
13. I am bothered by acid (sour) stomach several times a week.	*1. Yes 2. No 3. DK 4. NA
14. My memory seems to be all right (good).	1. Yes *2. No 3. DK 4. NA
15. Have you ever been bothered by "cold sweats"? Would you say: often, sometimes, or never?	*1. Often 2. Sometimes 3. Never 4. DK 5. NA
16. Do your hands ever tremble enough to bother you? Would you say: often, sometimes or never?	*1. Often 2. Sometimes 3. Never 4. DK 5. NA
17. There seems to be a fullness (clogging) in my head or nose much of the time.	*1. Yes 2. No 3. DK 4. NA
18. I have personal worries that get me down physically (Make me physically ill).	*1. Yes 2. No 3. DK 4. NA

	Item	Response
19.	Do you feel somewhat apart even among friends (apart, isolated, alone?)	*1. Yes 2. No 3. DK 4. NA
20.	Nothing ever turns out for me the way I want it to (turns out, happens, comes about, i.e., my wishes aren't fulfilled).	*1. Yes 2. No 3. DK 4. NA
21.	Are you ever troubled with headaches or pains in the head? Would you say: often, sometimes, or never?	*1. Often 2. Sometimes 3. Never 4. DK 5. NA
22.	You sometimes can't help wondering if anything is worthwhile anymore.	*1. Yes 2. No 3. DK 4. NA

BIBLIOGRAPHY

Ackerman, Nathan W. _Exploring the Base for Family Therapy_. New York: Family Service Association of America, 1961.

_____. _The Psychodynamics of Family Life_. New York: Basic Books, Inc., 1958.

Angell, Robert C. _The Family Encounters the Depression_. New York: Schribner's Sons, 1936.

Baldwin, Alfred L. _Theories of Child Development_. New York: John Wiley & Sons, Inc., 1968.

Becker, Howard, and Reuben Hill. _Family, Marriage and Parenthood_. Boston: D. S. Heath & Co., 1948.

Beisser, Arnold, and Norbert Glasser. "The Last Straws in Mental Illness." _San Francisco Chronicle_, March 22, 1970.

Bell, Robert R. _Marriage and Family Interaction_. Illinois: The Dorsey Press, 1967.

Bell, N. W., and E. F. Vogel (eds.). _A Modern Introduction to the Family_. Glencoe, Illinois: Free Press, 1960.

Blalock, Hubert M. _Methodology in Social Research_. New York: McGraw-Hill Book Company, 1968.

Blumenthal, Monica D. "Mental Health Among the Divorced." _Archives of General Psychiatry_, 16:603-608, 1967.

Bonjean, Charles M., Richard J. Hill, and Dale S. McLemore. _Sociological Measurement_. San Francisco: Chandler Publishing Co., 1967.

Bossard, James, and Eleanor S. Boll. "Family Ritual and Family Integration." Norman W. Bell and Ezra F. Vogel (eds.), _The Family_. Glencoe: Free Press, 1960.

Brayfield, Arthur H., and Harold F. Rothe. "An Index of Job Satisfaction," _Journal of Applied Psychology_, 35:307-11, 1951.

Brimm. O. G., Jr. _Socialization After Childhood_. New York: Wiley and Sons, Inc., 1966.

Broom, Leonard, and Phillip Selznick. Sociology. New York: Harper and Row, 1955.

Burchinal, L. G., G. R. Hawkes, and B. Gardner. "Personality Characteristics and Marital Satisfaction." Social Forces, 35:218-222, 1957.

Burgess, Ernest W., and Harvey J. Locke. The Family. New York: American Book Company, 1945.

Burgess, Ernest W., and P. Wallin. Engagement and Marriage. New York: Lippincott, 1953.

Campbell, Angus. "The American Way of Mating: Marriage Si, Children Only Maybe." Psychology Today, 8:37-43, 1975.

Cavan, Ruth Shonle (ed.). Marriage and Family in the Modern World. New York: Thomas Y. Crowell, Co., 1969.

_____, and Katherine Ranck. The Family and the Depression. Chicago: University of Chicago Press, 1938. Reprinted New York: Arno Press and The New York Times.

Charney, Israel W. Marital Love and Hate. New York: Macmillan Company, 1972.

Christensen, Harold T. (ed.). Handbook of Marriage and the Family. Chicago: Rand McNally & Company, 1964.

Clausen, John A. (ed.). Socialization and Society. Boston: Little, Brown and Company, 1956.

Crago, M., and R. G. Tharp. "Psychopathology and Marital Role Disturbance: A Test of the Tharp-Otis Descriptive Hypothesis." Journal of Consulting and Clinical Psychology, 32:328-341, 1968.

Cuber, J. F. "Three Prerequisite Considerations in Diagnosis and Treatment in Marriage Counseling." R. H. Klemer (ed.), Counseling in Marital and Sex Problems. Baltimore: Williams and Wilkins, 1965.

Cuber, John F., and Peggy B. Harroff. "The More Total View: Relationships Among Men and Women of the Upper-Middle Class." Marriage and Family Living, 2:140-145, 1963.

David, Gerson. Patterns of Social Functioning in Families with Marital and Parent-Child Problems. Canada: Toronto University Press, 1967.

Davis, Kingsley. Human Society. New York: The Macmillan Company, 1949.

Dean, Dwight G. "Alienation: Its Meaning and Measurement." American Sociological Review, 26:753-758, 1961.

deRam, Edith. The Love Fraud. New York: Clarkson N. Potter, Inc., 1965.

Dohrenwend, Barbara S. "Life Events as Stressors: A Methodological Inquiry." Journal of Health and Social Behavior, 14:167-175, 1973.

Dohrenwend, Bruce P., and Barbara Sneel Dohrenwend. Social Status and Psychological Disorder: A Causal Inquiry. New York: John Wiley, 1969.

Dohrenwend, Bruce P., Gladys, Engre, and Frederick Mendelsohn. "Psychiatric Disorder in General Populations: A Study of the Problem of Clinical Judgment." American Journal of Psychiatry, 127:40-49, 1971.

Dollard, John. "The Family: Needed Viewpoints in Family Research." Social Forces, 35:109-113, 1935.

Ehrenwald, Jan. Neurosis in the Family. New York: Harper and Row, 1953.

Eisenstein, Victor W. Neurotic Interaction in Marriage. Philadelphia: J. B. Lippincott Company, 1953.

Farber, Bernard. "An Index of Marital Integration." Sociometry, 1957.

_____. Family Organization and Interaction. San Francisco: Chandler Publishing Company, 1964.

Farson, Richard E., Phillip M. Houser, Herbert Stroup, and Anthony J. Wiener. The Future of the Family. New York: Family Service Association of America, 1969.

Folkman, Jerome D. "Stressful and Supportive Family Interaction." Marriage and Family Living, 18:102-106, 1956.

Gibb, J. R. "Defensive Communication." Journal of Communication, 3:141-148, 1961.

Glasser, Paul H., and Loi N. Glasser (eds.). Families in Crisis. New York: Harper and Row, 1970.

Gold, Herbert. "Divorce as a Moral Act." The Atlantic Monthly, 200:115-118, 1957.

Goode, William J. The Family. New Jersey: Prentice-Hall, Inc., 1964.

_____. World Revolution and Family Patterns. New York: The Free Press, 1963.

Gove, Walter R. "Relationship Between Sex Roles, Marital Status and Mental Illness." Social Forces, 51:34-44, 1972.

Haley, J. (ed.). Changing Families: A Family Therapy Reader. New York: Grune and Stratton, 1971.

_____. Strategies of Psychotherapy. New York: Grune and Stratton, 1964.

Handel, Gerald (ed.). The Psychosocial Interior of the Family. Chicago: Aldine Publishing Company, 1967.

_____, and Robert D. Hess. "The Family as an Emotional Organization." Marriage and Family Living, 18:100-101, 1956.

Hatch, David L., and Mary G. Hatch. "An Unhappy Family." Marriage and Family Living, 24:213-223, 1962.

Henry, Jules. Pathways to Madness. New York: Random House, 1971.

Hess, Robert D., and Gerald Handel. Family Worlds: A Psychosocial Approach to Family Life. Chicago: University of Chicago Press, 1959.

Hicks, Mary W., and Marilyn Platt. "Marital Happiness and Stability: A Review of the Research in the Sixties." Journal of Marriage and the Family, 32:553-574, 1970.

Hill, Reuben. Families Under Stress. New York: Harper, 1949.

Hill, Reuben, and Donald Hansen. "The Identification of Conceptual Frameworks Utilized in Family Study." Marriage and Family Living, 22:200-311, 1960.

Hogarty, Gerald E., and Marvin Katz. "Norms of Adjustment and Social Behavior." Archives of General Psychiatry, 25:470-480, 1975.

Holland, Davis. "Familization, Socialization, and the Universe of Meaning: An Extension of the Interactional Approach to the Study of the Family." Journal of Marriage and the Family, 32:415-427, 1970.

Hollingshead, August B. Two-Factor Index of Social Position. New Haven, Connecticut: Privately mimeographed, 1957.

_____, and Fredrick C. Redlich. Social Class and Mental Illness. New York: John Wiley & Sons, 1958.

Horney, Karen. The Neurotic Personality of Our Time. New York: W. W. Norton & Company, Inc., 1945.

Howells, John G. Theory of Practice of Family Psychiatry. New York: Brunner/Moyee, 1971.

Jansen, Luther T. "Measuring Family Solidarity." American Sociological Review, 17:727-733, 1952.

Jordan, William. The Social Worker in Family Situations. London and Boston: Routledge & Kegan, 1972.

Josselyn, Irene M. "The Family as a Psychological Unit." Social Casework, 34:336-343, 1953.

Kallman, F. "The Genetic Theory of Schizophrenia." C. Kluckhohn and H. A. Murray (eds.), Personality in Nature, Society and Culture. New York: Alfred A. Knopf, Inc., 1956.

Kerlinger, Fred N. Foundations of Behavioral Research. New York: Holt Rinehart and Winston, Inc., 1973.

_____, and Elazar J. Pedhazur. Multiple Regression in Behavioral Research. New York: Holt, Rinehart and Winston, Inc., 1973.

Kieren, Diane, and Irving Tollman. "Spousal Adaptability: An Assessment of Marital Competence." Journal of Marriage and the Family, 34:247-263, 1972.

King, Charles H. "Family Therapy with the Deprived Family." Social Casework, 48:203-208, 1967.

Klemer, R. H. "Treating the Patient's Marriage Problems: An Overview." R. H. Klemer (ed.), Counseling in Marital and Sexual Problems. Baltimore: Williams & Wilkins, 1965.

Landis, Judson T., and Mary G. Landis. Building a Successful Marriage. Englewood Cliffs, New Jersey: Prentice-Hall, Inc., 1948, 1963.

Langer, Thomas S. "A Twenty-two Item Score of Psychiatric Symptoms Indicating Impairment." Journal of Health and Human Behavior, 3:269-276, 1962.

_____, and S. T. Michael. Life Stress and Mental Health: The Midtown Study. New York: The Free Press of Glencoe, 1963.

Laws, Judith Long. "A Feminist Review of Marital Adjustment Literature: The Rape of the Locke." Journal of Marriage and the Family, 33:483-516, 1971.

Leighton, Alexander H. An Introduction to Social Psychiatry. Springfield, Illinois: Charles C. Thomas, 1960.

_____. My Name Is Legion. New York: Basic Books, Inc., 1959.

LeMasters, E. E. "Holy Deadlock: A Study of Unsuccessful Marriages." Ruth S. Cavan (ed.), Marriage and Family in the Modern World. New York: Thomas Y. Cromwell Co., 1969.

Lenski, Gerhard E. "Status Crystallization: A Non-vertical Dimension of Social Status." American Sociological Review, 19:407, 1954.

Lidz, Theodore. The Family and Human Adaptation. New York: International University Press, Inc., 1963.

_____, Alice R. Cornelison, Stephen Fleck, and Dorothy Terry. "Intrafamilial Environment of the Schizophrenic Patient: VI." The Transmission of Irrationality. Archives on Neurology and Psychiatry, 79:305-316, 1958.

_____. "The Intrafamilial Environment of Schizophrenic Patients: II. Marital Schism and Marital Skew." American Journal of Psychiatry, 114:241-248, 1957.

Linton, Ralph. Culture and Mental Disorder. Illinois: Charles C. Thomas, 1956.

Lipetz, Milton E., Lawrence S. Rogers, Harl H. Young, Irwin H. Cohen, and Jack Dworin. "Marital Stability, Mental Health and Marital Satisfaction." Journal of Consulting and Clinical Psychology, 35:342-348, 1970.

Locke, Harvey J., and Karl M. Wallace. "Short Marital-Adjustment and Prediction Tests: Their Reliability and Validity." Marriage and Family Living, 21:251-255, 1959.

Locke, Harvey J., and Robert C. Williamsen. "Marital Adjustment: A Factor Analysis Study." American Sociological Review, 23:562-569, 1958.

Loeb, J. "The Personality Factor in Divorce." Journal of Consulting Psychology, 30:562, 1966.

_____, and J. R. Price. "Mother and Child Personality Characteristics Related to Parental Marital Status in Child Guidance Cases." Journal of Consulting Psychology, 39:112-117, 1966.

Lorand, S. "The Role of the Psychoanalyst in Marital Crisis." S. Rosenbaum and I. Alger (eds.), The Marriage Relationship. New York: Basic Books, 1968.

Maccoby, Eleanor E., and Carol N. Jacklin. "What We Know and Don't Know About Sex Differences." Psychology Today, 8:109-115, 1974.

Manis, Jerome G., and Bernard N. Meltzer. Symbolic Interaction: A Reader in Social Psychology. Boston: Allyn and Bacon, Inc., 1972.

Manis, Jerome G., Milton J. Brawer, Chester L. Hunt, and Leonard C. Kercher. "Estimating the Prevalence of Mental Illness." American Sociological Review, 29:84-89, 1964.

Mathews, V. D., and Clement S. Mihanovich. "New Orientations on Marital Maladjustment." Marriage and Family Living, 25:300-304, 1963.

Mead, George H. Mind, Self, and Society. Chicago: University of Chicago Press, 1934.

Mechanic, David. Mental Health and Social Policy. Englewood Cliffs: Prentice-Hall, Inc., 1969.

Mechanic, David, and Edmund Volkart. "Stress, Illness Behavior, and the Sick Role." American Sociological Review, 26:53-55, 1961.

Meissner, W. W. "Thinking About the Family -- Psychiatric Aspects." Family Process, 3:1-40, 1964.

Miller, Daniel R., and Guy E. Swanson. The Changing American Parent. New York: Wiley, 1958.

Miller, Delbert C. Handbook of Research Design and Social Measurement. New York: David McKay Company, Inc., 1964.

Murstein, Bernard J., and Vincent Glaudin. "The Relationship of Marital Adjustment to Personality: A Factor Analysis of the Interpersonal Check List." Journal of Marriage and the Family, 28:37-43, 1966.

Myers, Jerome K., and Lee L. Bean. A Decade Later: A Follow-up of Social Class and Mental Illness. New York: John Wiley & Sons, Inc., 1968.

Myers, Jerome K., and Bertram H. Roberts. Family and Class Dynamics in Mental Illness. New York: John Wiley & Sons, Inc., 1959.

Nie, Norman H., Dale H. Bent, and Hadlai Hull. Statistical Package for the Social Sciences. New York: McGraw Hill Book Company, 1970.

Nye, Ivan F. "Child Adjustment in Broken and in Unhappy Homes." Marriage and Family Living, 19:356-361, 1957.

_____, and Felix M. Berardo. Emerging Conceptual Frameworks in Family Analysis. New York: The Macmillan Company, 1966.

Odegard, O. "Marriage and Mental Health." Journal of Mental Science, 92:35-59, 1964.

O'Neill, George, and Nena O'Neill. Open Marriage. New York: M. Evans and Company, Inc., 1972.

Otto, Herbert. "What Is a Strong Family?" Marriage and Family Living, 24:78-80, 1962.

Parad, Howard J., and Gerald Caplan. "A Framework for Studying Families in Crisis." Social Work, 5:3-15, 1960.

Parker, Beulah. A Mingled Yarn. New Haven and London: Yale University Press, 1972.

Parker, E. S., Prusoff, B. A., and Uhlenhath, E. H. "Sealing of Life Events." Archives of General Psychiatry, 25:340-347, 1971.

Parsons, T., and Bales, R. F., with Olds, J., Zelditch, M., and Slater A. Family, Socialization and Interacting Process. Glencoe, Illinois: Free Press, 1955.

Pavenstedt, Eleanor (Ed.). The Drifters: Children of Disorganized Families. Boston: Little, Brown and Company, 1967.

Perutz, Kathrin. Marriage Is Hell. New York: William Morrow & Company, Inc., 1972.

Phillips, Derek L. "The 'true prevalence' of Mental Illness in a New England State." Community Mental Health Journal, 2:35-40, 1966.

_____, and Segal, B. F. "Sexual Status and Psychiatric Symptoms." American Sociological Review, 34:58-72, 1969.

Prins, Sol A. "A Case of Conjugal Psychosis." Psychiatric Quarterly, 24:324-337, 1950.

Renne, Karen S. "Correlates of Dissatisfaction in Marriage." Journal of Marriage and the Family, 32:54-67, 1970.

_____. "Health and Marital Experience in an Urban Population." Journal of Marriage and the Family, 33:338-348, 1971.

Rogers, Carl. Becoming Partners: Marriage and Its Alternatives. New York: Delacorte Press, 1972.

Rose, Arnold M. "Alienation and Participation: A Comparison of Group Leaders and the Mass." American Sociological Review, 27:834-839, 1962.

Sarwer-Foner, S. I. "Patterns of Marital Relationship." American Journal of Psychotherapy, 17:31-44, 1963.

Satir, Virginia. Conjoint Family Therapy. U.S.A.: Science and Behavior Books, Inc., 1964.

_____. Peoplemaking. Palo Alto: Science and Behavior Books, Inc., 1972.

Schatzman, Morton. Soul Murder. New York: Random House, 1973.

Seeman, Melvin. "On the Meaning of Alienation." American Sociological Review, 24:783-791, 1959.

Seiler, H., and Summers, Gene F. "On the Relationship Between Physiological Malaise and Psychological Symptoms of Stress: A Male-female Comparison." Paper presented at the American Sociological Association Annual Meetings (August), New Orleans.

Seiler, Lauren H. "The 22-Item Scale Used in Field Studies of Mental Illness: A Question of Method, a Question of Substance, a Question of Theory." Journal of Health and Social Behavior, 14:252-262, 1973.

Shostrom, Everett, and Kavanaugh, James. Between Man and Woman. Los Angeles: Nash Publishing, 1971.

Shibutani, Tomatsu. Society and Personality. Englewood Cliffs, New Jersey: Prentice-Hall, Inc., 1961.

Skolnick, Arlene. The Intimate Environment. Boston: Little, Brown & Company, 1973.

Sroll, Leo, Langner, Thomas S., Michael, Stanley T., Opler, Marvin K., and Rennie Thomas, A. C. Mental Health in the Metropolis: The Midtown Manhattan Study, Vol 2. New York: McGraw-Hill, Inc., 1962.

Stryker, Sheldon. "Symbolic Interaction as an Approach to Family Research." Marriage and Family Living, 21:111-119, 1959.

Sussman, Marvin B. Sourcebook in Marriage and the Family. Boston: Houghton Mifflin Company, 1968.

Terman, L. M. Psychological Factors in Marital Happiness. New York: McGraw-Hill, 1938.

Tharp, Roland G. "Marriage Roles, Child Development and Family Treatment." American Journal of Orthopsychiatry, 35:531-538, 1965.

_____. "Psychological Patterning in Marriage." Psychological Bulletin, 60:90-117, 1963.

_____, and Otis, G. D. "Toward a Theory for Therapeutic Intervention in Families." Journal of Consulting Psychology, 30:426-434, 1966.

Turner, Ralph H. Family Interaction. New York: John Wiley & Sons, Inc., 1970.

Vernon, Glenn M. Human Interaction. New York: The Ronald Press, 1965.

Waller, Willard. The Family. New York: The Drysden Press, 1951.

_____. The Family: A Dynamic Interpretation. New York: The Cordon Company, 1938.

_____. The Old Love and the New. New York: Liveright, 1930.

Weinberg, Kirson S. The Sociology of Mental Disorders. Chicago: Aldine Publishing Company, 1967.

Younghusband, Eileen (ed.). Social Work with Families, Vol. 1. London: George Allen & Unwin Ltd., 1967.